PRAISE FOR
Discontent and Its Civilizations

"Hamid is an amazingly gifted writer and [*Discontent*] is a near-perfect essay collection, filled with insight, compassion, and intellect. It's a powerful look at the way people juggle their individuality with the tensions that inevitably result from being part of a community." —NPR

"Compelling. ... Reflect[s] the same subtleties of thought [as Hamid's novels], laid down in his lapidary, crystalline prose. . . . The chapters about Mr. Hamid's own life and his meditations on Pakistan's tumultuous recent history . . . command attention—and call out for a volume of their own." —Michiko Kakutani,
The New York Times Book Review

"Elegant, piercing, [and] often funny." —*Chicago Tribune*

"A deft and fluid novelist, unafraid to take on big topics . . . [Hamid] make[s] a case for the way big issues unfold across individual lives. And yet his intent is not to trace the evolution of the war on terror but how it alters us on the most intimate terms." —*Los Angeles Times*

"The author of three groundbreaking novels . . . [Hamid] compels readers to see the global need for empathy as well as the need to acknowledge that we are all hybrid beings. And it is this blended approach—personal essays bolstered by research . . . that makes Hamid's argument so successful. . . . [T]his book is essential . . . important and urgent." —*The Brooklyn Rail*

"Illuminating." —*O, The Oprah Magazine*

"Whether the essays are brief, evocative op-eds or longer essays on literature and Pakistan's history, they are always concerned, at their core, with the rippling impact of globalization . . . offering perspectives . . . that are little heard in the West. . . . No matter where we live, Hamid's insights are a testament to our shared responsibility and humanity." —*Biographile*

"[A] must-read." —*Condé Nast Traveler*

"Hamid's first three novels are canny, intimate reader-writer transactions . . . [In *Discontent*] he swaps that conferred 'you' for a confessional 'I'. . . . Powered by innate wisdom and informed opinion . . . the Hamid that emerges is a probing, critical political animal, one that is resistant to foreign intervention in Pakistan; anxious for more pluralism and tolerance within its borders; prepared to find good in the 'brutal phenomenon' that is globalization; and mystified—rightly—by 'illusory' civilizations." —*The Daily Beast*

"One of the most successful and inventive young novelists. . . . [In *Discontent*] his self-deprecating and witty tone is utterly engaging." —*The New York Review of Books*

"Whether writing about global politics or theories of narrative, Mohsin Hamid is that rare writer who's comfortable in both worlds. This collection of over a decade's worth of his nonfiction is essential, expansive reading." —Vol 1. Brooklyn

"Superb." —*Bookforum*

"Vivid, full of sumptuous aphorisms on the role art can play in life. . . . The author's best essays—like his fiction—shine by demolishing the boundaries." —*A.V. Club*

"The short, crisp essays in *Discontent* are empathic yet critical reflections on family, nationalism, sex, economics, Islamophobia, literature, violence, and other expressions of humanity. . . . Affable and concise, Hamid also proves he is a journalist capable of distilling politically charged conflict into a compelling, measured form . . . par[ing] his viewpoints to give readers not oversimplifications but, rather, perspective."   —*Shelf Awareness*

"Poignant and funny."   —Kojo Nnamdi, WAMU

"A mesmerizing read . . . Hamid seamlessly fuses the personal and the political . . . [his] perspective is essential to better understand our world."   —*The Progressive*

"Extremely insightful and illuminating."   —Book Riot

"Vital. . . . The essays' trenchant cultural commentaries and beguiling memory pieces illuminate Pakistan's present and past from both personal and political angles. . . . On almost every page, Hamid's mind is as fresh in its perspective and limber in its logic as in his fiction . . . [and] delivers a portrait of a country that's impossible to reduce to a tidy set of traits."   —*Oregon Live*

"Sharp . . . pithy [and] erudite."   —*Christian Science Monitor*

"Remarkable . . . thought-provoking, even entertaining . . . a collection to be savored and to be reread."   —About.com

"Perceptive and inspiring."   —*Harvard Crimson*

"[Hamid's] wise antipathy toward nationalism and religious fanaticism echoes loudly in a world riven by sectarian conflict. . . . He could despair of a country of 180 million people afflicted by terrorism, US drone attacks with a siege mentality toward India, and a predilection for military coups. Instead, he stresses Pakistan's elected assemblies, its free media, its independent judges, and the great potential of its people." —*Irish Times*

"[Hamid] is one of the most celebrated, inventive writers of the times." —Ozy.com

"Tearing down stereotypes and assumptions, Hamid gives an insider's look that is truly unique." —Brit & Co.

"An important writer, not just in his conversational style that combines his personal convictions and depth of knowledge, but also in vantage point." —Ask Men

"Smart doesn't begin to describe Hamid; he is the sort of thinker that could change hearts and minds." —*Booklist*

"Hamid's novels are concise literary gems . . . [and] *Discontent* suggests the potential for him to give us books of even greater importance, both literary and topical, for many years to come. And we will need him in those years, just as we need him now."
—EthanCasey.com

"In contrast with the debased language of extremism, militarism, and nationalism, [Hamid's] is a humane and rational voice demanding a better future." —*The Sunday Telegraph* (UK)

"Eloquently written and richly informed . . . For longtime Hamid readers, this is a great compilation for getting reacquainted . . . For new readers, it is an excellent introduction . . . [to] an intelligent and impassioned writer whose work deserves a wide readership." —*Library Journal*

"A heartfelt celebration of diversity and the power of the imagination." —*The Guardian*

"Honest and candid . . . Passion and hope infuse Hamid's most incisive dispatches." —*Kirkus Reviews*

"Give[s] a vivid sense of life lived close to the headlines. . . . [T]he recurring theme—that individuals matter more than the groups we try to assign them to—is as relevant as ever. And . . . the writing . . . is as simple, immediate, and moving as any of Hamid's fiction." —*Financial Times*

"Vivid touches . . . elevate Hamid's intelligent . . . commentaries above the commonplace . . . *Discontent* suggests Mohsin Hamid is reasonable, intelligent . . . and humble. In short, just the sort of commentator the world could do with right now." —*The Independent* (UK)

"*Discontent* . . . encourages us to look again at [Hamid's] growing body of work, personal and political, imaginary and reality based. It seems almost to invite us to observe the overlaps and discontinuities between the political viewpoints and subject matter that preoccupy Hamid in his nonfiction writing, and the literary perspectives and techniques he deploys in creating his novels. . . . After reading this latest collection, one is left to fantasize and project a vision of what may come next for [the author]." —DAWN.com

"Elegantly crafted essays confront everything from the future of Pakistan and the death of Osama bin Laden to fatherhood and falling in love. The insights into Hamid's literary style and influence will delight devotees of his work and intrigue newcomers. . . . Hamid makes a compelling case for pushing back against the mono-identities of religion, nationality, and race and for embracing the things that all human beings share." —*The Prospect* (UK)

Discontent *and* Its Civilizations

DISPATCHES FROM
LAHORE, NEW YORK,
AND LONDON

Discontent *and*
Its Civilizations

Mohsin Hamid

RIVERHEAD BOOKS
New York

RIVERHEAD BOOKS
An imprint of Penguin Random House LLC
375 Hudson Street
New York, New York 10014

The Library of Congress has catalogued the Riverhead hardcover edition as follows:

Hamid, Mohsin, date.
  Discontent and its civilizations : dispatches from Lahore, New York, and London /
Mohsin Hamid.
    p.   cm.
  ISBN 978-1-59463-365-2
  I. Title.
  PS3558.A42169A6   2015   2014027668
  814'.6—dc23

First Riverhead hardcover edition: February 2015
First Riverhead trade paperback edition: February 2016
Riverhead trade paperback ISBN: 978-1-59463-403-1

Printed in the United States of America
10 9 8 7 6 5 4 3 2 1

Book design by Marysarah Quinn

FOR DINA AND VALI

Contents

Art *81*

Politics *121*

Discontent *and*
Its Civilizations

My Foreign Correspondence

O NE DAY, beside a slender stream in the high mountains, a monk met an essayist and they fell to talking.
The minutes passed as they reclined there in the presence
of dragonflies. It soon seemed clear to the essayist that the
monk's view of life, perched as it was upon a foundation of
faith, was ripe for a good debunking.

The essayist laid out the required argument in painstaking
detail, ending with these words: "Since you have no proof, I
must conclude your beliefs are merely your own invention."

"So what?" the monk responded, with a smile as steady as
it was serene.

"So what? So everything. You're a monk!"

The monk hiked up the robe he was wearing and dipped
the back of one powerfully muscled calf in the water. "I in-
vented myself," the monk said. "Until yesterday I was an
Olympic sprinter."

The essayist stared, incredulous.

"Invention," the monk explained, "is a blessing."

GLOBALIZATION IS A brutal phenomenon. It brings us mass displacement, wars, terrorism, unchecked financial capitalism, inequality, xenophobia, climate change. But if globalization is capable of holding out any fundamental promise to us, any temptation to go along with its havoc, then surely that promise ought to be this: we will be more free to invent ourselves. In that country, this city, in Lahore, in New York, in London, that factory, this office, in those clothes, that occupation, in wherever it is we long for, we will be liberated to be what we choose to be.

When I sat down to shape this book, a collection of pieces I wrote for various publications in the fifteen years between 2000, the time my first novel, *Moth Smoke*, appeared, and now, which is to say 2014, I found I was content to let much of what I had written go. Many of my past pieces were, to my present eye, simply too crudely built or too blatantly wrongheaded to include. Others were too similar to each other, meaning it was better not to pick two when one would do.

What was left, the three dozen or so pieces making up the pages that follow, I wanted to alter as little as possible, so that they would read much as they read when they were first written. I have made some minor changes, probably the most significant of which are deletions of passages that seemed too repetitive, but I have done my best to avoid any major rewriting. Each of the pieces remains of its place and of its time.

Rereading them now, I am struck by how their writer, which is to say me, has changed over the years. Obviously, there have been changes in writing style and technique. But there have been other changes as well, changes in how I view the world, changes that perhaps reflect how I am in the world, and those changes remind me that I am becoming a different person, that I am inventing myself as I go along, as I suspect we all are. The novelist I am now would not today write the novels I wrote before; the human I am now might not behave as did the human I was before.

In that sense, the fragmentary and "of the moment" nature of the pieces that constitute this book brings with it, I hope, a different type of honesty than a book that is conceived as a whole and executed in a single effort. It reveals opinions and attitudes that are malleable, showing the plasticity of what in any given present moment one typically presents as a rock of certainty.

But it reveals consistencies, too, themes that reappear, again and again, in pieces written at different times, for different publications, in different places. Over the past fifteen years I have lived in three cities: Lahore, New York, and London. I have called and considered all three home. And yet, as I review the writings in this book, I recognize that I have always felt myself a half-outsider. The pieces here take different forms: some are lengthy essays, others are focused op-eds, others still are small fragments just a page or two long. But all of them, I think, are the dispatches of a correspondent who cannot help but be foreign, at least in part.

PAKISTAN EMERGES as a recurrent subject of mine. I have lived more of my life in Pakistan than in any other country, even if that total still comes to a little less than half. I am pre-occupied with Pakistan's future, as most Pakistanis I know seem to be, Pakistan being simultaneously an unusually trou-bled country and one that manages to provide many of its daughters and sons with remarkably resilient roots, roots that often endure even when the plant they belong to is removed to soil a vast ocean away.

In my writings about Pakistan over the years, I perceive an attempt at optimism, probably a little forced, and possibly somewhat misguided. I have often noted the potential for changes for the better that, in retrospect, have not occurred. And yet I think a stance of optimism is not useless. With opti-mism comes agency, the notion that Pakistan can solve its own problems. And a lack of agency has been at the heart of Paki-stan's failures, an impulse to blame foreign powers who, while very far from guiltless in the Pakistani context, have only sec-ondarily contributed to Pakistan's ongoing crises, which re-main primarily of Pakistani making. My position has been that foreign powers should resist the impulse to intervene in Pakistan, and that Pakistanis should correct failed Pakistani policies and attitudes themselves rather than claim these are the best that can be hoped for given the machinations of the outside world.

I think Pakistan matters, not just to myself and other Pakistanis, nor only because it is beset with terrorism and possesses nuclear weapons, but because Pakistan is a test bed for pluralism on a globalizing planet that desperately needs more pluralism. Pakistan's uncertain democracy and unsteady attempt to fashion a future in which its citizens can live together in peace are an experiment that mirrors our global experiment as human beings on a shared Earth. The world will not fail if Pakistan fails, but the world will be healthier if Pakistan is healthy.

Pakistan is at the forefront of the escalating conflict between Sunnis and Shias that is convulsing many Muslim-majority countries. Most Muslims worldwide are Sunnis, and acceptance by Sunnis of the rights of the largest Muslim minority group, Shias, is therefore a vital step toward building meaningful religious tolerance for all, including for targets of persecution such as Christians, Hindus, Ahmadis, secularists, and those of no religion.

Pakistan is also one of many places whose citizenry is made up of a patchwork of intermixed ethnic and linguistic groups—as are, for example, the European Union, Ukraine, Nigeria, South Africa, India, and Malaysia. Meeting the chal-

lenges of coexistence in societies like Pakistan will be critical
if the twenty-first century is to avoid repeating the bloody in-
ternecine wars of the twentieth.

Sadly, Pakistan's history these past fifteen years has not
been very promising. Religious and ethnic minorities have
been subjected to legal and political discrimination, targeted
assassinations, and, in some cases, a level of violence tanta-
mount to wholesale slaughter. Even more worrisome, in its
resistance to pluralism, Pakistan's trajectory has been far from
unique.

I HAVE LIVED in Pakistan during its recent and most intense period of terrorist activity and drone strikes, in London
during the years on either side of the 2005 public transport
bombings, and in New York in the era that came to an end
with the attacks on the World Trade Center of 2001—and so
it is perhaps not surprising that what has been called "the war
on terror" features centrally in these essays. Indeed, this entire
collection might be read as the experience of a man caught in
the middle of that conflict.

To my mind, the "war on terror" is not, at its heart, an
actual war. Yes, it has involved wars in Afghanistan and Iraq.
And it has involved violence of various types and intensities
in innumerable other places: Pakistan and Britain, America
and Russia, Libya and Yemen, India and Indonesia, Spain and
Kenya—the list goes on and on. But wars, insurgencies, cross-

border raids, and terrorism characterized the twentieth century, too. What distinguishes the "war on terror" is that it is a war against a concept, not a nation. And the enemy concept, it seems to me, is pluralism.

Pakistan and other Muslim-majority countries have hardly been unique in their struggles to accommodate diversity. In the United States and Europe, the "war on terror" has been accompanied by a great backlash against migrants. Actual walls are being constructed along the southern border of the US, with drones deployed overhead, and some American states are legislating draconian anti-migrant restrictions. Anti-migrant parties are in the ascendant across the EU, and Britain is considering leaving the bloc, in large part because of anger over migrants.

In many places, the past fifteen years have been a time of economic turmoil and widening disparities. Anger and resentment are high. And yet economic policies that might address these concerns seem nearly impossible to enact. Instead of the seeds of reform, we are given the yoke of misdirection. We are told to forget the sources of our discontent because something more important is at stake: the fate of our civilization.

Yet what are these civilizations, these notions of Muslimness, Western-ness, European-ness, American-ness, that attempt to describe where, and with whom, we belong? They are illusions: arbitrarily drawn constructs with porous, brittle, and overlapping borders. To what civilization does a Syrian atheist belong? A Muslim soldier in the US army? A Chinese professor in Germany? A lesbian fashion designer in Nigeria? After how many decades of US citizenship does a Spanish-speaking Honduran-born couple, with two generations of American children and grandchildren descended from them, cease to belong to a Latin American civilization and take their place in an American one?

Civilizations are illusions, but these illusions are pervasive, dangerous, and powerful. They contribute to globalization's brutality. They allow us, for example, to say that we believe in global free markets and, in the same breath, to discount as impossible the global free movement of labor; to claim that we believe in democracy and human equality, and yet to stymie the creation of global institutions based on one-person-one-vote and equality before the law.

Civilizations encourage our hypocrisies to flourish. And by so doing, they undermine globalization's only plausible promise: that we be free to invent ourselves. Why, exactly, can't a Muslim be European? Why can't an unreligious person be Pakistani? Why can't a man be a woman? Why can't someone who is gay be married?

Mongrel. Miscegenator. Half-breed. Outcast. Deviant. Heretic. Our words for hybridity are so often epithets. They shouldn't be. Hybridity need not be the problem. It could be the solution. Hybrids do more than embody mixtures between groups. Hybrids reveal the boundaries between groups to be false. And this is vital, for creativity comes from intermingling, from rejecting the lifelessness of purity. If there were only one human left, our species would die.

WHEN I WAS YOUNGER, I thought of being a migrant and being foreign as things that made me different, an outsider. Now, at the age of forty-three, I think these experiences are increasingly universal.

On our globalizing planet, where the pace of change keeps accelerating, many of us are coming to feel at least a bit foreign, because all of us, whether we travel far afield or not, are migrants through time. Even if you are eighty and have never left your hometown, yours has become another country from that of your childhood.

Perhaps, as we search for principles that can bind together our diverse and interconnected world, we should explore the empathy that arises from such a shared experience. It may be that as we examine our position as temporal beings, as individuals who represent a folding together of days, years, and decades—as a person who is at once a child of the seventies, say, and a mother of the noughties—a sense of our common hybridity may start to become apparent. To be a human being and to be a hybrid being are the same thing.

In my writing, I have tried to advocate the blurring of boundaries: not just between civilizations or people of different "groups," but also between writer and reader. Co-creation has been central to my fiction, the notion that a novel is made jointly by a writer and a reader. Co-creation is central to my politics as well. I believe that we co-create the overlapping societies we belong to, large and small, and that we should be free to try to invent new ways of being and interacting.

At some level, I suppose my personal need to write fiction comes from my inability entirely to accept our world as it is. When I write a novel, I am disappearing into another world, one of my own devising. But I don't desire to remain there, alone, apart, forever. I want to bring my imagined world back into our world, to share it, to have a reader enter it and shape it, to open a space for experimentation and imagination that crosses the boundaries of the self, of the real, of time. I believe that the hope of invention animates the arts. And I feel that same hope as I think of people coming together to invent a world that is post-civilization, and hence infinitely more civilized.

THIS BOOK IS ORGANIZED into three sections: life, art, and politics. This is not because I hold these categories to be separate: I think the opposite, that the personal is political and vice versa, and my own art partakes strongly of both. Rather, the structure here is intended as a possible journey.

The pieces in the first section, titled "Life," are arranged in subsections that adopt the age-following order of chapters in a memoir. The second section, "Art," is divided into subsections more thematically. And the final section, "Politics," is composed of subsections that retain the basic chronology of when the pieces were written, and therefore tracks the evolution of my perspective, starting in 2000 and ending in the present.

I wanted the experience of reading this book to be like developing a relationship. The first section would allow you, the reader, to get to know me a little; in the second section, you would see how I think about and approach the task of writing; and in the third, you would encounter me writing some opinions on the world we share.

All that said, you, too, have been on your own path of invention these past fifteen years. You, too, are a foreign correspondent in your own right. So how (and whether) you now proceed is, of course, up to you. That's the thing about co-creation. To exist, it requires the presence of more than one point of view.

LIFE

1

Once Upon a Life

Art and the Other Pakistans

When Updike Saved Me from
  Morrison (and Myself)

In Concert, No Touching

Once Upon a Life

IN DECEMBER 1980, at the age of nine, I moved back to Pakistan for the first time.

We touched down at Lahore, in those less security-conscious days when it was still a place where families strolled to the tarmac to greet deplaning passengers. Ronald Reagan had just beaten Jimmy Carter in the election for president of the United States, the Soviet Union was about to mark the first anniversary of its invasion of Afghanistan, racoon-eyed General Zia-ul-Haq was ensconced in Islamabad as Pakistan's dictator, and I'd lost my Urdu.

It's a funny thing to lose your first language. I was an early talker, chirping along in full sentences and paragraphs well before I turned two, and I have a scar to prove it. In the summer of 1973, Zulfikar Ali Bhutto was campaigning to become prime minister of Pakistan, and I picked up the habit of climbing onto the dining table and holding forth in the manner of the speeches I'd heard him make on PTV: "When I become prime minister . . ."

One day someone tried to get hold of me and lower me to the ground. I made a run for it, dashed into thin air, fell, split open my head, and wound up with blood in my eye and stitches across my brow. (Z. A. Bhutto's fate would, sadly, be similar.)

The following year I left Lahore, winging via Hong Kong and over the Pacific to San Francisco with my parents. In California we moved into one of many identical graduate student town houses on the Stanford University campus. Bands of kids ran around and chased butterflies and dashed through the *tish-tish-tishing* rotating water sprinklers, all barefoot, unsupervised. I slipped out to join them.

My mother heard crying and went to investigate. She saw me in tears at the door next to ours, gazing up at a perplexed neighbor, surrounded by jeering children. My mother took my hand and led me back home.

"Is he retarded?" one of my new playmates asked her.

"No," she answered.

"Then why can't he talk properly?"

"He can. He just doesn't know English."

After that I didn't speak for a month. My parents worried, but they decided I probably just needed time to adjust. So they let me sit in front of our TV, do my drawings, and build precariously tall towers with my wooden blocks. And when I next spoke, much to their surprise, it was in English, in complete sentences, and with an American accent.

Over the next six years I didn't speak a word of Urdu. I made friends, went for sleepovers, brought home tadpoles and frogs in jam jars, ran like the wind, played soccer, crashed out on unused beds at grad student parties, camped in tents in national parks, asked what that funny smell was at a spliff-heavy open-air Bob Marley concert, swam in the frigid Pacific, dressed in moccasins and beaded vests, and wrote my first stories—intergalactic space operas inspired by a slew of sci-fi movies and TV shows of the time: *Star Wars, Star Trek, Battlestar Galactica, Buck Rogers, Space Ghost, Star Blazers, Battle of the Planets.*

Meanwhile, my dad did his PhD, my mom worked in the accounting department of an early Silicon Valley electronics firm, my little sister was born, and our battered second-hand Datsun clocked tens of thousands of miles.

I'd been so fluent in Urdu, and such a talker, that my parents never realized just how completely I'd forgotten the language until we arrived back in Pakistan.

I was thrown into a strange new (old) world of extended families, aunts and uncles, two dozen cousins, cricket, odd-tasting bread, still-odder-tasting milk, only one television channel—and even that on for only part of the day—and an almost complete absence of familiar consumer brands. Here in Lahore there were no Frosted Flakes, Twinkies, Nestlé Quik, Trapper Keepers, Nerf balls, Bactine, no No More Tears shampoo.

On my first day in Pakistan, I asked a cousin, "Are these people slaves?"

"No," he explained. "They're servants."

I kept wanting to write to my friends in California but never managed to. What would I even say? Months passed and then it seemed too late. One night I looked up at the stars and thought these were the same stars people over there looked up at, and I cried. It was the only time. Pretty melodramatic stuff. But it passed.

Or maybe it didn't, but it did subside. Besides, I made new friends, learned new sports, biked around town, found a place that sold model airplane kits, another that sold aquariums and tropical fish, and understood—after the first few bruises—that my cousins were actually like brothers and sisters, a classroom-sized clan always ready to chat and play and come unquestioningly to my defense against the outside world.

I liked my new existence, but I'd liked my old one, too, and I imagined places where the two could come together. I was a map buff, and for my tenth birthday my parents bought me an exquisite atlas. Pencil in hand, I would create new countries: nonexistent Pacific islands with snow-topped volcanoes and tightly packed contour lines, the French department of Alpes-Maritimes as an independent republic (I admired its shape), the Kathiawar peninsula separated from the mainland by a deep canal, a confederacy of midsized city-states scattered across a variety of continents.

I would write the almanac entries for these places, their histories and natural resources and climates and militaries and flora and fauna. And, importantly, their demographics: always mixed, with no clear majority, and significant immigrant groups of Lahori and San Franciscan descent.

This was the creative writing initially inspired by my return to Pakistan. (There was also some poetry, modeled on verses in Tolkien and in *Bulfinch's Mythology*. "Do you know what a virgin actually is?" my dad asked me upon reading it. "Like a maiden?" I ventured.)

Most of my family and classmates in Lahore spoke English, so I didn't need to fall silent this time. I just started picking up Urdu on the go. Eventually I could tell a joke and sing a song in it, flirt and fight, read a story and take an exam. I could speak it without a foreign accent. But my first language would be a second language for me from then on.

English fractured for me, too, coming in distinct Californian and Pakistani varieties. (Later, in adulthood, Mid-Atlantic and British English would be added to my mix.)

Sometimes, as a nine-year-old twice transported, the words I heard moved me in unexpected ways, like impressions of half-forgotten sunny afternoons, less than memories and therefore impossible to share.

I wonder now if that is partly why I write, to try.

(2011)

Art and the Other Pakistans
(The Ones That Don't Make the Headlines)

LOOKING BACK, it's obvious to me now that the Pakistan of my teens was bursting with art. I had a burly cousin who used to play (incongruously) with inks and watercolors in the afternoons when he got home from school. I had an aunt who was in the habit of telling over and over again the story of her random encounter with the famous artist Sadequain, an encounter that resulted in him executing what was surely his version of an autograph: a quick drawing depicting my aunt as a Nefertiti-necked goddess holding a flower above a line of calligraphy. I had seen the legendary painter Chughtai's long-eyed ladies smiling out from drawing room walls, offering half-lidded innuendoes to easily flustered young men like me. And I had in the backdrop of my youth the Lahore Museum, the marvelous old city, the trucks and cinema billboards covered in bold, pelvis-thrusting iconography.

But at the time, art felt to me like something that belonged either to the past or to other places, because my teens were in the 1980s, and Pakistan in the 1980s had the misfortune of being governed by a mustachioed dictator with dark bags under his eyes and a fondness for dystopian social reengineering. General Zia-ul-Haq claimed to be acting in the name of Islam, and even though the history of Islam in our part of the world stretched back over a thousand years, we were told that our Islam wasn't Islamic enough, indeed that we Muslims weren't Muslim enough, and that he would make of our Pakistan the "land of the pure" that its name suggested—or ruin us all trying.

Under Zia, flogging, amputation, and stoning to death became statutory punishments. Acts disrespectful to symbols of Islam were criminalized. Public performances of dance by women were banned. News in Arabic, the language of the Koran but spoken by virtually no one in Pakistan, was given a prime-time slot on television. Thugs belonging to the student wings of religious parties seized control of many college campuses. Heroin and assault rifles flooded the streets, "blowback" from Pakistan's alliance with the United States against the Soviets in Afghanistan. My parents reminisced about how much more liberal Lahore had been in their youth.

When General Zia was blown to bits shortly after my seventeenth birthday in 1988, he wasn't mourned, at least not by anyone I knew. I left for college in the United States a year later. There I met people who were studying photography and sculpture, and I myself enrolled in classes on creative writing. Without thinking about it, I supposed an education in these

"artistic" pursuits was something in which only affluent societies in the West could afford to invest, or, rather, that only the
twin luxuries of material success and tolerance of free expression could provide the sort of soil in which an artistic education could thrive.

I was, of course, completely wrong. When I returned to
Pakistan in 1993, I was working on what would become my
first novel. I thought of writing as a transgressive act. I wrote
at night, often from midnight to dawn, and in between writing sessions I would escape into the darkness with my friends.
We drove around town in old Japanese cars, hung out on our
rooftops, and searched for places beyond the reach of societal
control or parental observation. Cheap local booze and even
cheaper slabs of hash were the intoxicants of choice in that
young urban scene, and avoiding the predations of the bribe-
taking police was an alarming and amusing preoccupation.

Increasingly I found my wanderings taking me into the
world of the National College of Arts. A couple of my friends
were enrolled there, one studying architecture, another
graphic design. Others were dating students: painters, print-
makers. It was unlike anything I had ever seen. Students of all
social classes, and from all parts of Pakistan, attended NCA.
The place was a microcosm of Pakistan, but of a creative Pakistan, an alternative to the desiccated Pakistan General Zia
had tried to ram down our throats. Here people who prayed
five times a day and people who escaped from their hostels late

at night to disappear on sexual adventures in the city could coexist. In the studios I saw calligraphy and nudes, work by students with purely formal concerns, and by others for whom art overlapped with politics. I was inspired. I wrote like crazy. I made friends I have kept for life.

Love comes to mind when I think of that time. There was a lot of it going on among the people I hung out with. But I was also falling in love with Pakistan. I have always had a stubborn affection for the land of my birth. When I went abroad for college, I thought I knew it pretty well. But it was my encounters with the denizens of the NCA universe after my return that reminded me that Pakistan is too vast a country to be known, that it is full of surprises, of kinks and twists, of unexpected titillations and empathic connections, of a diversity that can only be described as human. It was exciting and vital and real.

Or rather, *they* were exciting and vital and real—for my Pakistan had become plural. The art, and artists, I found at NCA ushered me into many more Pakistans: the nascent underground music scenes, the emerging film and television scenes, the scenes of writers like myself, and of course the scenes of other art and other artists, not just in Lahore but in Karachi and Islamabad and elsewhere, and not just in 1993 but in the rest of the nineties, the noughties, and now.

Just a few months ago I was in Amsterdam with two old friends from the Lahore art world. On a warm summer night we checked out some galleries and walked along the canals, whirring bicycles and shrooming teenagers passing us in the darkness. Nothing could have been more different from where we had all been fifteen years earlier. And nothing could have been more similar, either.

(2009)

When Updike Saved Me from Morrison (and Myself)

O NE DAY IN the spring of 1993, Toni Morrison took me out for lunch. It was my last semester at Princeton, and I was in her long-fiction creative writing workshop. I'd done two semesters of short story work with Joyce Carol Oates, and I hoped to be a novelist. So I was writing fast. I think we had to produce thirty or forty or fifty pages for Toni. I'd hit a hundred and was still going.

We sat and chatted and ate (what, I don't remember, but it included fries). I told her I'd got into law school. I told her I was planning to take time off first, to head back to Pakistan and write. I told her I'd been cooking for myself that year. I told her I made a mean pasta and she ought to give it a try. Really? she said. Yeah, I said. I invited her down to the basement kitchen of Edwards Hall and told her she wouldn't be disappointed.

To my surprise, she said she'd come. It better not be over-boiled spaghetti in some sauce out of a can, she warned me.

I smiled. Confident. As we left the restaurant she noticed a paperback hidden between notebooks and printouts in my hands. She asked me what it was. I told her it was *Jazz*. She asked if it was the first of hers I'd picked up. I confessed it was. She signed it for me. Then she said, Read *Beloved*, it's good.

I still remember how she said it: *good*. Drawn-out. Beautiful and powerful, the way words she spoke often were. When she read our stuff out loud to us in class, it sounded like literature. So I picked up *Beloved* next. And she was right. It was good.

I thought I was pretty good myself back then. I thought the novel I was writing was good. I thought my cooking was good. I was twenty-one years old and didn't know better, thank goodness. And luckily for me, Toni never showed up for that pasta.

Instead, I got a message on my answering machine from her assistant. Toni couldn't make it that day, sadly. John Updike (I think it was Updike) had come to campus. I hadn't yet read Updike but the name sounded familiar. I called back and said no problem.

It wasn't until later that it occurred to me my cooking might not have been quite as good as I thought it was. My pasta was indeed spaghetti. It was probably overboiled. And while the sauce didn't come out of a can, it did come out of a bottle. All I really did was add some hot chilis to it. And maybe a couple of other spices. But maybe not.

Why I was so proud of it, I can't for the life of me recall.

As for the novel I was writing, I finished a draft for her class. Toni liked it enough to ask me to read from it at the annual end-of-year creative writing event. I still have a manuscript with several pages of her exquisitely fountain-penned suggestions on the reverse. I figured I was almost done.

It wasn't ready for publication for another seven years.

(2009)

In Concert, No Touching

IT WAS WHEN I returned to Pakistan soon after college that a woman introduced me to the pleasures of sweat.

The scene was a religiously inspired, eternally ongoing Sufi dance/trance event. For the uninitiated reader, I would liken this to an open-air rave, but with free admission, and music generated solely by hand drums and bells on the anklets of long-haired male dancers, some of whom were in drag.

As with any rave, the audience included the sick in search of healing, couples desperate for fertility and not a few pot smokers puffing on joints that flavored the air like wands of tuberose.

I had come at ten-thirty because this was when Papu Sain unleashed the kinds of rhythms many believed could take you closer to God.

I was in need of sensual indulgence. At home, a combination of tradition, respect, and the unpopularity of contraceptives meant that any young man returning from college abroad might find himself self-reliant in the act of love to a degree unknown since his dimly recollected boys' school past.

In my case it would be more honest to blame shyness and bumbling ineptitude. But whatever the cause, I found female companionship limited in those days to my family and the girl-friends of my more fortunate friends. This lack in my life was compounded by a general concealment of the female form itself, Lahore lagging behind New Jersey in the display of skin. Satellite television and imported magazines, with images of women for the most part physically rather unlike those around me, created an ache with no obvious cure in the region.

So I adapted. I developed a taste for subtlety, for the micro-ripples that are the tsunamis of a reduced-stimulus environment.

I learned to appreciate a smile, a brush of the hand. I studied eyes. I chose my words carefully and savored those I was given.

And it was with this, the heightened sensitivity born of necessity, that I found myself standing at Baba Shah Jamal only three feet from a woman my age. Her veil covered her throat and the rear hemisphere of her head like a motorcycle helmet with the visor up. Her clothing was as loose as love, enough to make a full body slim and a slender one curve. It swelled at her chest and hips.

I watched her pick her nose delicately with her thumb. She noticed my gaze, and we both turned to look ahead with the self-conscious expression of people whose attention is centered in their peripheral vision.

It was hot.

And together, we sweated.

I felt myself shiver as my pores opened, gaping fish mouths on a desert beach. Warmth issued from my body. Perspiration gathered in the close-cropped hair at the bottom of my scalp.

The unexpected fingernail of a trickle followed my spine, and my guts tightened, a quick exhalation at the shock. Her face had begun to shine. She wiped her mouth with her wrist. I felt another caress along my ribs, touching the damp flesh of my flank. My thoughts expanded into the air and condensed on her skin. A slow lick descended from my armpit.

Together, we surrendered to it, the wet stroking of our bodies building as we stood quietly apart. Beneath us men whirled in ecstasy. Shutting her eyes and looking up, she displayed the underside of her jaw in a mating dance as old as time, a peahen glancing coyly at the hip-flashing merengue of a peacock.

Thick drops slid down my belly like errant salmon roe.

I risked a smile at her with my eyes fixed on the scene below. A sly glance only half blocked by my nose revealed the side of her mouth responding, stretching out toward me in langorous recline.

There is a simple code about these things: your intentions must be honorable. To go any further, you should have love on your mind. We didn't, so we didn't.

But we sweated, and when she left without a word, I was not ungrateful.

(2001)

2

International Relations

—

The Countdown

—

A Home for Water Lilies

International Relations

THE PASSPORT I hand through the slit in her glass shield runs suspiciously backward, the right-hand cover its front, and above the curved swords of its Urdu lettering she reads, "Islamic Republic of Pakistan." Words to make a visa officer tremble.

The scene is the Italian consulate in New York, the back entrance, a subterranean room staffed by three polite sentries. They are charged with the defense of a wall that runs around wealthy democracies, and their post is less tense than many because it lies inside the fortifications of an ally.

I am well dressed. A navy suit, pinstriped, three-buttoned. White shirt, blue tie, brown face, brown eyes. I shaved this morning but missed a patch beside my chin. The stubble there, though short, is dense. Fundamentalist stubble. Ayatollah, Hez-bollah stubble. Fighting in the heights of Kashmir stubble. But just a hint.

In uncalloused hands, marred only by cuticles in need of a

lesson, I hold my remaining documents: letter from employer, bank statement, proof of insurance, recent pay stub, airline ticket, hotel booking. A mother could arrange a marriage with less information than I am asked to present. My eyes are shadowed with stress or lack of sleep. I am sweating slightly, despite the coolness of this day, and my scalp glistens where the hair has forsaken it.

My smile is dishonest, the smile of a man who hopes his smile will make it easier for him, insincere as attempts at sincerity tend to be. She is almost friendly in return. We are both young, after all, healthy members of the same species and of breeding age.

There are only a hundred and one points to the inspection a Pakistani must pass to be deemed travel-worthy. I fail—because I have succeeded in the past. I have traveled to Italy too often.

Why so many trips over so short a period? she asks.

Love, I say. My girlfriend is Italian.

She pauses, not eager to do this. But she must: it is her duty. The wall is only as strong as its weakest gate.

Yes, that is a very good reason, she says. But I am afraid we will need proof: a notarized letter and a copy of her passport.

You need a letter from a woman confirming our relationship? I ask.

The visa officer is human. Humane. She blushes. I am afraid so, she says. But I will approve your application now so you do not have to make an extra trip. Just bring the letter with you when you come to pick up your visa. Please do not forget: you will be asked for it.

I know I am fortunate. She could, at her discretion, have turned me down. Other visa officers in other consulates regularly reject my kind for far less. Still, I am not pleased.

My colleagues in our business-casual office were amused that I wore a suit that day, but I was ashamed. It tacitly acknowledged an accusation I would have liked proudly to ignore. But what exactly is the accusation?

Race has become too clumsy a shorthand for the legal boundaries that divide liberal democracies such as the United States. Nationality, unless overcome by wealth, is a far more acceptable proxy. Nations deemed prone to poverty and violence are walled off to consume themselves, to fester. And nationality-based discrimination has taken its place alongside racial discrimination, denying both our common humanity and our unbelievably varied individuality as it frisks us at the border.

Here, in cosmopolitan New York, I am able to reside only at the sufferance of my employer, halfway through a six-year H-1B work visa, which binds the legality of my presence in the United States to my job. The Department of Labor and the INS are kept so understaffed that it currently takes several years for most green card applications to be processed. I could face eventual deportation even if I submit my petition today.

Like much of the indentured workforce, I feel insecure. I must produce notarized love letters at checkpoints. My category is not a desirable one.

But I do as I am told, and I am given my Italian visa.

I get into a cab and head back to my office. My driver looks like a terrorist: steady eyes, thick beard, the reserved watchfulness of the devout. A verse of the Koran dangles beneath his rearview. He could be my uncle.

Where are you coming from? he asks me in Urdu.

I was applying for a visa, I tell him.

You have had a hard morning, brother, he says, turning off the meter. This ride is on me.

(2000)

The Countdown

M Y PARENTS WENT out for dinner in Islamabad the other night. They sat among tables of foreign journalists who chatted about the war they had come to cover. My mother was frightened. She told my sister to consider leaving Pakistan. My sister refused.

She just graduated from college in June, from NYU as a matter of fact, and she loves her job. She does not intend to give it up. She is working on a television promo for the South Asian Federation Games, due to be held soon in Islamabad. The games may now be canceled, but in her office people are still trying to stay on deadline and on budget.

My sister says you just have to be careful. Stay away from public places, avoid large gatherings. Because people say the country may tear itself in two. Recently, in the mosque near our house, there was a calm appeal to support the Afghans. They are desperately poor, it was said, running out of food and fuel for heat in the coming winter. Less temperate voices have called for civil war if the government supports America in an attack on Afghanistan. And the Taliban have moved troops to the border.

People in Pakistan were not awakened to the possibility of violence by a surprise attack that claimed the lives of thousands of unsuspecting innocents. Instead, they have been forced to watch it coming from far off on the horizon, as they read the news about New York and Washington and waited for the reverberations of these distant tragedies to reach them. In that period of mounting dread, there were polite phone calls between heads of state and orderly airport closings. The embassies and multinational corporations sent home dependents and nonessential personnel. Twenty-four-hour news stations showed the gathering of carrier battle groups, special forces, aviation fuel. People had time to see their lives changing.

Perhaps because she stays at home when my father and sister go to work, my mother now seems the most frightened of the three. She is normally a woman of impeccable poise, so I find it unsettling to hear her voice slip from steady on the phone. "We could go," she says. "But what about your aunts and uncles and cousins? Not everyone can leave. So everyone stays." She tells me she attended a peace rally and watched as a small group of bearded protesters passed by, accompanied by a much larger flock of journalists. "It was as if they were the Beatles," she says. Despite everything, my mother has not lost her ability to be amused.

She watches television, still surprised that famous correspondents she has seen reporting from Bosnia and Somalia are now standing in front of buildings near the house. "I have complete sympathy for the Americans," she says. "It is terrible, what happened. But now they are so angry. They talk about a war on terrorism. But they never seem to think what they do terrifies normal people here."

I can remember seeing my father afraid only once, when I was in hospital as a child, before I underwent surgery for a vicious case of sinusitis. But having seen him then, I can imagine how he looks now—his lips a bit pale, more wrinkles in his forehead. "Nothing is happening," he says. "The shops are empty. The streets are quiet. Even the police seem few and far between. But every night we turn on the television, and we see what is coming. We just have no idea what it will mean for us."

Having no idea makes them nervous. An explosion brought my sister running from her bathroom. My parents reassured her the sound was only thunder. My sister, of course, claims she was not afraid. "The first few days, it was pretty bad," she says. "But then a week passes and you say, I can't wait forever. So you get on with it. I guess that must be a little bit like what people are doing in New York."

She used to live on Thompson Street, only a few blocks from my place on Cornelia. "You know," she considers, "I'm glad I'm not in New York now. When the attack happened, I almost wished I were there. I still felt more like a New Yorker than someone from Islamabad. But now I hear how scared my

Pakistani friends are, the abuse they're getting, and I'm glad I'm not there. I don't want to remember New York that way."

So my family waits, like many families in Pakistan, watching battle plans being discussed on television, ex-guerrillas being interviewed about the Afghan terrain, radical figures threatening bloodshed if Pakistan helps America. Meanwhile, the long summer has come to an end in Islamabad. The city is green and bougainvilleas are blooming. Fresh pomegranates are arriving from nearby orchards, along with grapes and apples. The fruit, which rarely makes the news, still makes people smile.

(2001)

A Home for Water Lilies

SINCE LEAVING MY birth city of Lahore at the age of eighteen, I had not lived in any one place for more than four years. So when I arrived in London in July 2001, I did not expect to stay long. The previous week, at my farewell and thirtieth birthday party in New York, I entrusted my battered pair of JBL speakers to a friend. I had purchased them on my first day of college, and had carried them from city to city like ancestral silver.

"Take good care of them," I told him. "I'll be back in twelve months."

"You never know, buddy boy," he said.

My friend, a Lahore-born nomad like myself, had a theory about us. We spoke Urdu, cooked mutter keema, danced the bhangra, regularly overslept; we had roots. And yet we drifted. So he called us water lilies, after a plant rooted not in dry earth but in ponds and streams. It was a rather unmacho sobriquet (unlike, say, "masters of the universe") but accurate nonetheless.

I landed in London, like so many foreigners, looking for a London that did not exist. Or rather, I was looking for London to express in its whole something that was true only of tiny parts of it. Where were the thugs who would casually call me "Paki" to my face? Where were the accents of Higgins and Pickering? Where were the casks of warm beer, the weekend cricket matches?

The flat above mine was occupied by an American woman, the one below by a French-Italian couple. The waiters at the nearest café were eastern European; the manager at the off-license was Sri Lankan. The city was more white than New York, but ethnically it seemed similarly varied.

I was far from falling in love at first sight. No, London and I began by exchanging a reserved handshake. My chameleon skin was still tinged with the gunmetal hues of New York, and I found London more expensive, quiet, and slow. I missed the energy of my old abode, with its nocturnal howls and incessant exhortations to strive for extreme and rapid success.

Then things changed. The 9/11 attacks placed great strain on the hyphen bridging that identity called Muslim-American. As a man not known for frequenting mosques, and not possessing a US passport, I should not have felt it. But I did, deeply. It seemed two halves of myself were suddenly at war.

For a time, my fiction floundered in the face of world events, so I turned to journalism and essays instead. I wrote a piece for a US publication about the fears of my parents and sister in Pakistan as the US prepared to attack Afghanistan. The paper deleted a paragraph on reasons for the anger felt toward America in many Muslim-majority countries. A similar piece I wrote for a British newspaper was published unedited and in its entirety.

This was my first experience of what I would come to recognize as growing American self-censorship. It was also the first time I became aware of the relative openness of the British press. I began to read more and more of what was being printed in London; I was surprised and impressed. As a writer, I found the atmosphere in London liberating, not just because of what I was reading, but because of the debates I overheard at the office and at neighboring tables in restaurants. My fiction began to flow again. When the end of my one-year work assignment in London arrived, I arranged to have it extended indefinitely.

The longer I stayed, the more London grew on me. I discovered the Ain't Nothing But . . . blues bar on Kingly Street, the Lahore Kebab House in the East End. In the late winter of my second year, I marched with a million people to Hyde Park to protest against the impending invasion of Iraq. Looking around me, especially at grandparents with their grandchildren, I found myself thinking: "I am one of them. I am a Londoner."

This was a disturbing thought, given my predilection for wandering, so I quickly pushed it away. Intellectually and politically, I had found much to admire in London. And yes, I could have a good time. But my heart was still closed; Lahore had been my first love and New York my most passionate affair. London and I, I thought, were destined to be just friends.

Then, one August afternoon in my third London year, London introduced me to my wife. I met her outside a pub in Maida Vale. She and I had been born on the same street in Lahore. We were strangers. We chatted in the sun beside the canal, agreed to meet for dinner. A week later, she returned to Lahore.

We dated long-distance, an exciting and near-bankrupting experience of transcontinental flights, prepaid calling cards, and garbled Internet telephony. Two years later we were married.

London taught me the pleasures of being a husband. Restaurants, museums, cinemas, pizza delivery, late-night video-on-demand: these things acquired entirely new romantic hues. We went for hour-long walks at midnight, gave directions to tourists. We found we could always get a table, even on a crowded night, at the Churchill Arms.

And so, after five years of living here, I find myself beginning to commit to London in completely unexpected ways. For the first time in my life, I am looking to buy a flat. Not because I dream of getting rich off my investment, but because I dream of staying.

The friend who has my old JBL speakers has now moved from New York, via Vancouver, to Amsterdam. I have never asked for the speakers back, but I often tell him that he ought to give this city a try.

There is something magical about London. It can coax a water lily to tie its roots to land.

(2006)

3

Down the Tube

—

On Fatherhood

—

It Had to Be a Sign

Down the Tube

Last June, on a hot day in London—hot enough to remind me of Lahore—I got on the Tube and found myself in a crowded carriage with one empty seat. Nobody moved to take it, which seemed strange because several people were standing. Then I noticed the fellow in the next seat over. He was, I guessed, of Pakistani origin, with intense eyes, a prayer cap, a loose kurta, and the kind of mustacheless beard that tabloids associate with Muslim fundamentalists. He could have been my cousin.

Look at this racial profiling, I thought to myself. Here's this fellow, perfectly harmless, and everyone's staying clear like he's planning to kill them. And then they wonder why Muslims in Britain feel ostracized.

I took the seat, gave the fellow a smile that meant, "Hello there, brother, we're on the same side," and opened my copy of *The Economist*. And that would have been that.

Except that it wasn't, because once the doors slammed

shut and the train jerked forward, he said, disconcertingly loudly, "Why do Arabs get all the credit?"

I wasn't sure what to make of his question, so I said, "Excuse me?"

He jabbed his finger at the cover of my magazine. It carried a photograph of Abu Musab al-Zarqawi, by reputation a particularly nasty Jordanian militant, killed a few days previously in Iraq.

"Why do Arabs," he said again, almost shouting, "get all the credit?"

I observed that he had earphones on, the small fit-in-your-ear iPod variety, and also that people had started staring at us.

"I'm not sure I know what you mean, friend," I said, forcing another smile onto my face. Then I added, "I'm from Pakistan myself."

I added this because I wanted to make sure he understood the connection between us. I also added it because he was acting a little oddly and I figured that if he actually was a terrorist he might be less likely to blow himself to smithereens if he thought he was sitting next to another Muslim.

His eyes began to leap from me to the magazine, to the window, to me again. Over and over. It occurred to me that we were getting rather close to the first anniversary of the 7/7 bombings. Didn't terrorists have a thing about anniversaries?

"And where are you from?" I said coaxingly. Distract him. Keep him talking. Establish a rapport.

"I'm in the security business. Get it? The security business.

My own company. And I like music. I bought a system for ten thousand pounds."

Okay, then. This fellow clearly wasn't flying on all four engines. And he was nervous. He was sweating like a Swede in the Sahara. And what was that? Yes, he had a bulge under his kurta. Like a money belt. A very, very large money belt.

Play for time. "I'm a bit of a music fanatic myself," I said. I winced inwardly at my unfortunate use of the word "fanatic," then went on. "I have this old Carver power amp. Bought it way back in '93 or '94. Just the sweetest sound."

He took his earphones off, slowly, and glared at me. I watched his every move. I wasn't the only one. And I got the feeling that we had a few eavesdroppers as well. Like that woman reading Jamie Oliver upside down.

Then he said, "I'm on medication, did you know that?"

"Er, no. Are you . . . all right now?"

"STOP TALKING TO ME!"

Now we had everyone's attention. "Sure. Okay. Sorry."

He put his earphones on again. I observed him, James Bond–like, out of the corner of my eye. I wondered how he would trigger the explosives. Would he raise his arm, relying on a hidden detonator built into his sleeve? Or would he have to reach under his kurta and press a button on the bomb itself?

I readied myself for action. I ran kung-fu moves through my mind, super-slow, at *Matrix* special-effects speed. I would have to grab him, pin his arms to his sides, and hold on while squealing like a schoolgirl for help.

He looked at his watch. So did I. Five o'clock. And not just five o'clock. Exactly, to the second, five o'clock. This was it.

The train started to slow. We were pulling into a station. My station. Just a few more moments. Maybe I would make it.

Nothing happened. We arrived, the doors opened, and he and I simultaneously rose and exited onto the platform. I stood and watched him walk away, wondering if I should say something. He was perhaps the most suspicious person I had ever seen in my life.

But remembering my own experience of "random" searches and multihour detentions at immigration lounges around the world, I thought of what might happen to the fellow if I mentioned him to the authorities. He would be stopped. He would act strangely. Even if he was completely innocent, which he probably was, he might well resist being questioned. And then, through no fault of his own, he might find himself under arrest.

I couldn't set in motion that sequence of events. So I did nothing, and I hoped I would not discover on the television later that evening that my inaction had made possible a slaughter.

Stepping into the open air, I found my friend, who was visiting me from Pakistan, and told him the story of what had just happened.

He laughed. "You're just paranoid, yaar," he said. "You've been living here too long."

(2006)

On Fatherhood

I NEVER REALLY THOUGHT of myself as a baby person. Children I liked. Children you could talk to, hang out with. My own inner child was alive and well. But babies, the larval, pre-talking, pre-walking form of humanity, had little appeal to me. Yes, babies could look cute. But I'd been in enough relationships to know looks only go so far, particularly when they're packaged with a high-maintenance need for constant attention.

Then I had one. My baby daughter was born last year. Her name is Dina. About thirty minutes after she arrived in the world, her mother, my wife, was taken off for post-labor surgery. My mother-in-law, traumatized after witnessing her child give birth, was recovering her composure in the hospital courtyard, chain-smoking cigarettes between rounds of prayer. So the nurse handed Dina to me. And then we were alone.

Dina was swaddled in white, lightly streaked in dried

blood and other bodily fluids. She weighed seven and a half pounds. About the same as a small dumbbell. But she wasn't as dense as a dumbbell, so she was bigger, maybe two-thirds the size of a two-liter bottle of soda. She rested in the crook of my arm. I did my best not to move.

Dina breathed. I breathed. We were silent. Then she started to cry. It wasn't a powerful sound. It was a small, quiet sound. It made me think of lungs that had been squeezed on their way through the birth canal, little wet lungs only just introduced to air.

I had no idea what to do. I couldn't lactate, so feeding her wasn't an option. I didn't know if I was holding her properly, whether I should be rocking her or keeping her still. But I felt her cry in my arms and I wanted to comfort her.

I talked to her. I told her who she was and who I was. I told her where her mother had gone and that she should be back soon. I told her it must be strange for her to go from being a sea creature to a land creature so suddenly. I told her I loved her, surprised as I said it that even though I'd known her less than an hour, it was true.

She stopped crying. I spoke some more. Then I fell quiet. Minutes passed. She cried again. I spoke again. She stopped. The cycle repeated itself. It seemed shocking each time. She cried, and I doubted if my speaking to her would make a difference, but again and again it did.

Later my wife told me that Dina probably found my voice soothing because she'd spent months hearing it in the womb.

So when I spoke, it was something familiar, and it reassured her. That was a reasonable enough explanation. But ever since that second half hour of her life, I felt Dina and I shared a bond. She had bumped me out of the center of my world.

I'd become a baby person, and it felt good, better than what had come before.

(2010)

It Had to Be a Sign

MY WIFE, Zahra, and I recently decided to move back to Pakistan. Many friends in London seem puzzled by our decision. That is understandable. Pakistan plays a recurring role as villain in the horror subindustry within the news business. It is, we are constantly told, a place where car bombs go off in crowded markets, beheadings get recorded in grainy video, and nuclear weapons are assembled in frightening proximity to violent extremists.

August 14 is Pakistan's independence day. This year it also marked the birth of our daughter, Dina. (It was a close thing. Nineteen hours later and she would have been born on India's independence day. For a novelist, the symbolism would have been considerably more tricky. Fortunately Dina was in no mood to dally.)

Childbirth changed my perception of my wife. She was now the bloodied special forces soldier who had fought and risked everything for our family. I was the supportive spouse tasked with cheering her victory, celebrating her homecoming, and easing her convalescence. So I gave her a respectful few hours before suggesting that we uproot our lives and move across continents to a city thousands of miles away.

If we were waiting for a sign from the universe that now was the time to return to our native Lahore, I told her, then Dina's arrival was surely it.

Zahra regarded me steadily from her hospital bed. She said she was unaware that we had been waiting for such a sign. I promptly agreed to her suggestion that we defer the conversation for a month.

This period allowed me to reflect. London had been good to me. It was eight years since I'd arrived, intending to stay one year, and I was still here. I'd met my wife in London. I'd written and published my second novel in London. I'd had my first child in London. London had given me friends, family, and—after two decades of part-time fiction writing—the ability to make a living from prose.

Like many Bush-era self-exiles from the United States, I found that London combined much of what first attracted me to New York with a freedom America seemed to have lost in the paranoid years after 9/11. The international border at Heathrow felt more permeable than the one at JFK; the London broadsheets were more open to dissenting voices and more resistant to patriotic self-censorship than newspapers in the US; and the naturalization process in the land of Buckingham Palace was—much to my surprise—considerably less tortuous than in the land of the Statue of Liberty.

Of course the UK had problems. Race relations was one. As a Pakistani friend who had also arrived here from America once pointed out to me: Dude, in this place *we* are the African Americans. Another was the strange support for institutionalized aristocracies—including, to my mind, such related phenomena as the monarchy, a tax system of unequal benefits for the "non-domiciled" resident rich, and an economic model dependent on a financial services industry whose participants privatize the profits of risks borne publicly.

All in all, however, the UK was a home in which I thrived, and London was a wonderful and quite amazing city.

But my heart remained stubbornly attached to Pakistan. I wore a green wig to the Twenty20 Cricket World Cup final at Lord's last summer. And although I left Lahore at eighteen to study abroad, the city of my birth never lost its grip on me. I continued to go there often, usually for two or three month-long trips every year and a couple of yearlong stays each decade.

Above all, I never believed in the role Pakistan plays as a villain on news shows. The Pakistan I knew was the out-of-character Pakistan, Pakistan without its makeup and plastic fangs, a working actor with worn-out shoes, a close family, and a hearty laugh.

Yes, these are troubled times for the country. Friends of

mine in Lahore tell me their children have not gone to school in three weeks because of fears of a Beslan-style terrorist atrocity. The university where my sister teaches has been installing shatterproof window film. Hundreds of people have been killed in attacks on Pakistan's cities since the army launched its operation in Waziristan last month.

But there are reasons to be positive, too. After a long history of backing religious militants, the state and army may finally be getting serious about taking them on. The Swat valley was successfully wrested from Taliban control this summer. The Waziristan offensive is said to be proceeding well. Pakistani public opinion has hardened against the extremists, and at the same time an increasingly independent media and judiciary are amplifying popular demands for a redistribution of resources to the poor. It is possible that out of the current uncertainty and bloodshed a more equitable and tolerant Pakistan will be born.

So when, a month after Dina's arrival, Zahra and I again discussed Pakistan, we decided to go. Given the peripatetic nature of my life so far, I don't know how long we'll stay there. Maybe a year, maybe ten, maybe forever.

But I do know this. When it comes to where we hope Pakistan is heading, we are voting with our feet.

(2009)

4

Avatar in Lahore

—

Don't Angry Me

—

Personal and Political
  Intertwined

Avatar in Lahore

ON THE DAY I went to see *Avatar* I finally got a haircut. I don't have much hair, but still I usually have myself cropped every three weeks. This time six had gone by, and I was looking scraggly.

It was January 2010, a month since I'd moved back to Lahore after several years in London and before that several more in New York. The week I arrived a pair of bombs went off in Moon Market, killing 42 people and injuring 135.

For a few days people avoided markets and banks and restaurants and other crowded places if they could. Then things more or less went back to normal. There were 8 million people in Lahore before the bombing. There were 8 million people in Lahore after the bombing.

I held off on going for a haircut. Maybe I was too busy settling in.

My barber wasn't in Moon Market. He was in Main Market. Main Market differs by two letters from Moon Market. Main Market is four kilometers away from Moon Market. Main Market is also larger and more densely packed than Moon Market.

The front of my barber's shop is a big glass window with some fading posters on it. On the narrow street outside are rows of parked motorcycles and cars. Bombs in Pakistan are sometimes left in motorcycles and cars. A bomb outside my barber's shop would turn that big glass window into shrapnel.

Eventually my wife pointed out that my hair really needed attention. So I went for my haircut. I hadn't seen my barber in years.

"Hot or cold?" he asked me.

"What do you mean?" I said. What the hell was a hot haircut? Or a cold one for that matter?

"Hot or cold?" he repeated, a little surprised.

I realized he was offering me tea or a soft drink. "Neither," I said, shaking my head. "Sorry, I've been away awhile."

He cut my hair. Then he gave me a scalp massage. Then he gave me a shoulder massage. He was good. I thought of staying longer. I looked at the big glass pane of the window and the cars and motorcycles parked outside. I paid him and left.

I'd had a number of missions since moving to Lahore. I'd had to get us a new fridge and sort out the strange smell coming from one of our bathroom drains and shepherd the cardboard boxes of our belongings through customs at the dry port. But my top priority had been getting broadband. I'd succeeded remarkably easily.

Now when I went online at home, thanks to a 1,999-rupee (roughly $23) monthly contract, I flowed at 2 Mbps through a Pakistan Telecommunications Limited ADSL telephone line, down to Karachi, offshore to the SEA-ME-WE-3, SEA-ME-WE-4, and I-ME-WE, a trio of optical fiber underwater cables that handle the bulk of data moving between South Asia and the Middle East and Europe, and thence to any server or router I needed to access on the planet.

Out in the cyber universe, my Internet persona could continue to live pretty much the same life it had lived when my physical existence was in London or New York. It could visit the same websites, follow the same news, correspond with the same friends and agents and publishers. This pleased me.

I'd been able to watch a streaming high-definition trailer for *Avatar* before going to see it that night.

When we arrived at the cinema, barricades meant that no one could park outside. We had to leave our car in a vacant plot down the road. A police jeep was stationed near the entrance. Security guards manned a metal detector. Inside, each bathroom had a guard as well. Other than that, it was like going to a modern Hollywood-dependent cinema anywhere. There was sweet and salty popcorn, there were hot dogs and nachos, there were M&M's and Coke.

The cinema was not configured for 3-D. But the screen was large and the surround-sound system was powerful, so the 2-D experience was still impressive.

The audience cheered as a race of exotically named, technologically disadvantaged, religiously inclined, dark-skinned (well, blue) people fought a marauding, resource-hungry, heavily armed force of seemingly American marines whose leader roared of the need to "fight terror with terror."

A friend leaned over to me when it was done. "Is James Cameron secretly Pakistani?" he asked.

We stepped outside. Some people smoked cigarettes. Others smoked joints. Then we drove home. I passed an army checkpoint on my way. At an intersection a digital billboard was running a news ticker with the number of deaths from the latest drone attack.

The main character in *Avatar* is a marine who goes online to inhabit a hybrid body that looks like the dark-skinned enemy. I wanted to get home to go online and explore his fictional universe further. I also wanted to get home because the streets were oddly deserted. A winter fog had descended, making it difficult to see ahead.

(2010)

Don't Angry Me

Passing through the Qatar airport, I thought I glimpsed, on the horizontally scrolling news ticker of a red-liveried news channel that was probably BBC, the information that an American ambassador had been killed. My first thought was, Where? My second, related, was, I hope not in Pakistan.

After reconfirming that my four-month-old son was securely strapped to my chest, I fished out my BlackBerry. Like many online Pakistanis, I have a group of friends I turn to for breaking news, political commentary, and gallows humor. My circle, mostly aged forty or thereabouts, favors the decidedly uncool (to which a chart of RIM's plummeting share price will, sadly, attest) medium of BlackBerry Messenger—BBM—for this purpose.

Responses to my BBM query were more or less instantaneous. "Not sure you read that right, bud." "Nope. Nothing on CNN." And then: "Wait. Ambassador down. Benghazi. Libya."

Libya. Surprising. I powered off my phone for the flight to Lahore. When I powered it up again, waiting my turn at the X-ray scanners with which customs officers prevent alcohol from being smuggled into Pakistan (the war on booze being approximately as successful in our country as the war on drugs is in the US), there were already several BBM messages suggesting that the ambassador's killing was related to the film *Innocence of Muslims*.

The following day, on BBM, Twitter, Facebook, and elsewhere, I came across numerous claims that we would soon see antifilm protests raging across Pakistan; questions about what was wrong with, variously, the Americans, the Libyans, us Pakistanis, Muslims, and the people who run YouTube; and jokes too offensive to too many varied sensibilities to consider reproducing here, although some were, in my admittedly idiosyncratic estimation, really quite good.

I also received more than the usual quantity of chain-SMS messages that day, and—in addition to the standard advertisements for English-language training courses, dengue-thwarting mosquito nets, energy-efficient air conditioners, and pay-by-text Koranic guidance—there were two that caught my eye.

The first read precisely as follows:

ALLAHU AKBAR!!!! The cinema in America that was going to play the film of the Prophet today at noon. An earthquake hit that area that caused the building to split into two pieces. The Americans are so shocked at the miracle, that they didn't allow full media coverage on the topic and that's why you didn't hear about it on the news today! Share this around and let people know that ALLAH is protecting the Prophet!!! PASS THIS MESSAGE ON! Please don't let this stop at your phone!

The second message called for a Pakistani boycott of Google, claiming (correctly) that Google owned YouTube, and also (correctly) that YouTube hosted video footage of the anti-Islam film, and, further, that Google earned five billion dollars in revenues in Pakistan (surely incorrect, despite the oft-reported statistic that we Pakistanis are among the world leaders in online searches for porn; Google's total global revenues are in the neighborhood of forty billion) and therefore that a Pakistani boycott would bring Google to its knees.

Whatever the merits of these bottom-up, user-driven responses to the affront, it was soon apparent that neither the Pakistani state nor opportunistic Pakistani fringe politicians, who lurk in the nether region where the plankton mist of perceived persecution meets the vent of ready violence, would allow this moment to be left to the conscience of mere individuals.

The state's reactions were immediately apparent. YouTube was blocked. The Internet throttled to a crawl. I have three broadband providers for my home, a bit obsessive, admittedly, but even in regular times the reliability of each leaves something to be desired. My cable modem promptly died. No Internet traffic could make its way in or (as far as I could tell) out. My DSL link was barely alive, operating at a speed that brought to mind the "boing boing" sound of an old dial-up connection. My WiMAX setup, normally the least fleet-footed of my three, the backup for my backup, dipped to about a quarter of its promised bandwidth, which, given the circumstances, wasn't bad. Unfortunately for me and my fellow Pakistani Web surfers, the state's online response also included, in a scattergun attempt to block specific IP addresses that might link to the film, the erection of a national firewall that denied access to what seemed like half the Web.

Fringe politicians were not far behind. Perhaps smarting from the recent Rimsha Masih fiasco—in which they had championed the execution of a fourteen-year-old mentally disabled Christian girl for the crime of blasphemy, only to be roundly rebuffed by a rare confluence of sane elements within Pakistan's legal system, media, civil society, and clergy, who collectively revealed that she had been framed by a property-coveting local mullah—they were eager to fan the momentarily sputtering violently righteous religious flame.

The protests they instigated gathered force. Two people had already died. In today's Pakistan, tragically, this is not uncommon. But there was a sense that things would intensify. Like weather channels giddy on the news of a menacing tropical depression, the local media reported an increase in emotional wind speed. Shouting politicians announced the formation of a telltale eye at the center of an anti-anti-Islam-film hurricane. It would, all agreed, make landfall on Friday, after the weekly communal prayer.

This also happened to be my three-year-old daughter's first week of school. She cried every morning as we dropped her off, apparently a sign of healthy attachment, though easily mis-construed (by me) as an indication that some great barbarism was being perpetrated.

So I was upset when the government declared Friday a public holiday, and not just any public holiday—Pakistan's (and possibly the world's) first Love the Prophet Day. The last thing my daughter needed was a three-day weekend just as she was beginning to settle in.

Views here were split. Some commentators lambasted the supposedly liberal, supposedly left-of-center Pakistan Peoples Party–led government for ceding space to extremists, for in effect declaring Love Burning and Looting and Pillaging Day, for not having the gumption to stand up and say that no matter how offensive the film, no one had the right (or indeed any reason) to kill one's fellow Pakistanis over it, to destroy public property, as would certainly happen, or to bring anarchy onto our streets. Surely the real problem that needed to be ad-dressed was one of faulty logic, what might be termed a "some-one has made a hateful film in America so now I ought to get shot by a Pakistani police officer" fallacy.

Others thought that the government had acted wisely, or at least shrewdly, in getting ahead of the curve, possibly co-opting the mounting indignation and reducing the potential for confrontation.

Still others thought that the government was a bunch of American/Zionist/Indian lackeys no matter what public holidays they declared, and that they deserved to burn in hell along with the filmmakers and, presumably, anyone else who happened to be in the wrong place at the wrong time on Friday.

My daughter was pleased that she would have a "day off"— after a life total of four days on.

The hurricane approached. People began their preparations. We did our grocery shopping on Thursday evening (the streets were packed; the traffic was terrible). My driver, a Christian, asked if he could stay home from work (the answer was yes). The birthday party of one of my daughter's classmates was canceled.

I woke up at seven a.m. on Friday. It was quiet. It isn't always quiet at our house. We can usually hear rumbling trucks and sputtering rickshaws and sometimes the shrieks of motorcycle daredevils as they race by, pulling wheelies. When the Sri Lankan cricket team was attacked in 2009, the automatic-weapon fire was clearly audible here. When bombs were going off more regularly a couple of years ago, the blast wave of one of them was powerful enough to rattle the windows.

Today there were birds chirping. And my phone had no

signal. The government had turned off mobile-telephone networks as a precaution. (Mobiles are occasionally used as detonators for explosives and, more commonly, for communications among militants during their operations.)

Fortunately BBM works over Wi-Fi, and those of us in my chat group who had functioning Internet at home (about half of us) were able to keep each other abreast of the latest developments. One reported that a sign saying "Death to Sam and Terry" had gone up on Lahore's main British-era thoroughfare, the Mall. I could guess who Sam was: Sam Bacile, a pseudonym of the hated filmmaker. But who, I asked, was Terry? "Florida preacher," came the response. "Koran-burning day."

The hurricane hit. On my TV set, Pakistan was aflame. E-mails from friends abroad asked after my well-being. I went out for a drive in the afternoon and things in my neighborhood were utterly calm—disconcertingly so, for mine is normally a bustling area to which the word "calm" does not usually apply. This reinforced the idea that Pakistan is a big country. A hundred and eighty million people is a lot of people. Pitched battles between protesters and police can be going on in one place, barriers made of shipping containers can be breached by mobs in another, and cinemas can be burned to the ground in a third—all of which did occur that day—and yet, in most locales, with the naked eye, you will see none of this.

Phone service was restored that night. Blogging, text messaging, op-ed-page comment posting, etc., resumed in earnest on Saturday. By most accounts, approximately twenty people had been killed across the country: rioters, police, a TV cameraman, bystanders. Among my Lahori friends there was an air of sadness, depression. Others were more proactive, like the five thousand students who signed up to coordinate cleanup efforts in Islamabad, Lahore, and Karachi through their dedicated Facebook page and the Twitter hashtag #Project CleanUpForPeace.

One friend sent, via BBM, a picture he had just taken of a rickshaw with these words written, in English, on the back of its fabric-covered cabin: "Don't Angry Me."

It was probably a reference to a popular Bollywood film. But I was reminded of the Gadsden flags I had seen flying, years ago, on a trip to South Carolina: bright yellow, with a rattlesnake and a warning, "Don't Tread on Me." Who knows, maybe the rickshaw driver had come back home from the United States after 9/11. Or maybe he'd stumbled upon that slogan, popular during the American revolution, on Google. Or maybe he'd even caught it in a clip, on a slow-buffering visit to YouTube, fluttering in the crisp breeze of freedom.

(2012)

Personal and Political Intertwined

WHEN I WAS writing my first novel, *Moth Smoke*, I tried to use imagery to reveal the mental state of the main character. It doesn't rain because a character is sad, of course, but a sad character, or so my thinking went, is more likely to notice the rain—and therefore, while narrating, to comment upon it.

My next novel, *The Reluctant Fundamentalist*, was in many ways quite different from its predecessor, but it, too, asserted a link between interior and exterior worlds. The notion that the personal and the political are inescapably intertwined was one I continued to hold strongly.

It was early in the process of working on my third novel that I moved back to Lahore, where I had grown up. The year was 2009. I had spent much of the 1990s in New York, writing about the Lahore of *Moth Smoke*. I had spent much of the 2000s in London, writing about the New York of *The Reluctant*

Fundamentalist. Now, I thought, I would try my hand at living in a country and writing about it at the same time.

So, as I ruminate on the not-yet-four years I have spent in Pakistan, on how the country has changed and evolved over this time, I find myself questioning my impressions. How much, I wonder, is the Pakistan that I see actually a reflection of my own life? How much of what I imagine to be its changes are in reality merely echoes of my own moods, my emotions?

Pakistan has just seen the first elected civilian government in its history complete a full five-year term. Its raucous press is increasingly assertive, as is its rather idiosyncratic Supreme Court. The army has mostly stood back, choosing not to intervene (yet) as it has so many times in the past. These are all promising developments.

The economy, however, has deteriorated since I returned. The rupee has plunged against the dollar, inflation continues to tug the prices of foodstuffs ever higher, and power shortages have reached the point where often we have electricity for no more than one hour of every two.

Law and order is bad. An insurrection rages in Balochistan. Killings of Shias across the country are getting worse. Ahmadis, Hindus, Christians, and other religious minorities are frequently targeted by violent bigots. A liberal governor of my province, Punjab, was assassinated. The houses of hundreds of Christians in my home city of Lahore were burned by a mob. I meet more and more Pakistanis abroad who say the persecution has grown so bad they would never consider returning.

But on university campuses, I meet thousands—literally thousands—of students who are bright, keen, and eager to learn. They seem to be reading novels. At least half of them are—unprecedentedly for Pakistan—female. I was told last year that there are more students enrolled in universities in Pakistan today than the total number who graduated in the five decades following independence in 1947.

I'm amazed by the talent of young musicians I hear at underground jam sessions, of young artists I see displaying their work. I'm encouraged by the young writers I meet. And the young readers. At the first-ever Lahore Literary Festival, held in February, the turnout was said to be twenty-five thousand. It was breathtaking. I can think of perhaps no public occasion in my twenty years as a novelist that I have enjoyed more than the talk I gave there.

Things in the country around me these past few years have been mixed. Much is horrible, much is beautiful, and much is in between.

Whether I see things accurately, though, I do not know. My own life has had its share of highs and lows, and like a character in one of my books, it may well be that the environment I perceive around me is but an echo of what I feel within. (Or equally, perhaps, the reverse might be true.)

I have, after two decades of mono-generational London and

New York living, been reintroduced to a multigenerational daily existence. My wife and I live with our two children in an apartment above my parents' house. Three generations at one address, as was the case when I was a child.

There is wonder in this, at seeing, for example, my daughter playing with her grandfather in the garden each morning before he goes off to teach at his university and she goes off to study at her nursery school. There is melancholy, too, in watching a generation of my aunts and uncles age, their numbers exceeding those of my generation, the cousins still living in Lahore.

Ours is a large extended family: my mother is one of nine, my father one of four. Every so often one of us is robbed, or taken to hospital, or forced to depend on others for economic survival. And we are, by far, better off than most.

Yet there is wisdom here, and love, and a measure of peace that descends between the times of upheaval. I have been planting trees along the perimeter of our house. For shade, and to keep the crowding city somewhat at bay.

(2013)

ART

5

Pereira Transforms
—
My Reluctant Fundamentalist

Pereira Transforms

I AM SOMETIMES ASKED to name my favorite books. The list changes, depending on my mood, the year, tricks played by memory. I might mention novels by Nabokov and Calvino and Tolkien on one occasion, by Fitzgerald and Baldwin and E. B. White on another. Camus often features, as do Tolstoy, Borges, Morrison, and Manto. And then I have my wild card, the one I tend to show last and with most pleasure, because it feels like revealing a secret.

Sostiene Pereira, I say, by Antonio Tabucchi.

These words are usually greeted with one of two reactions: bewilderment, which is far more common, or otherwise a delighted and conspiratorial grin. It seems to me that *Pereira* is not yet widely read in English, but holds a heroin-like attraction for those few who have tried it.

My own Pereira habit began a decade ago, in San Francisco's City Lights bookstore, where an Italian girlfriend suggested I give it a try. San Francisco was the perfect place for my first read: its hills and cable cars and seaside melancholy were reminiscent of *Pereira*'s Lisbon setting; its Italian heritage, from the Ghirardelli chocolate factory at its heart to the wine valleys surrounding it, evoked *Pereira*'s Italian author; and its associations with sixties progressivism and forties film noir went perfectly with *Pereira*'s politics and pace.

I have always had a thing for slender novels, and I liked the way *Pereira* looked, the way it felt in my hands. I took it back to my hotel, and straight to bed, at that unadventurous age still my preferred place for a read. It lay elegantly on the sheets beside me. I ran my thumb along its fore edge, narrow and sharp against my skin. I lifted it, opened it, and plunged in.

That first reading spanned a single afternoon and evening. I made it from cover to cover, pulled along relentlessly.

I was transfixed by *Pereira*'s beauty. In its compression it approached perfection. It swept me off to Lisbon in the thirties, to a "beauteous summer day, with the sun beaming away and the sea-breeze off the Atlantic kissing the treetops, and a city glittering, literally glittering" beneath a window. I developed a crush on the character of Marta, so briefly sketched, who in her "straw hat" and "dress with straps crossing at the back" asks Pereira to dance, a waltz he performs "almost in rapture, as if his paunch and all his fat had vanished by magic."

Despite its economy, *Pereira* was never perfunctory. It conjured out of its small hat a vast and touching sense of the humane. When the eponymous protagonist, an elderly and overweight journalist, confides each day in the photograph of his dead wife, I experienced their relationship as a living thing. When he tells her the young man Rossi is "about the age of our son if we'd had a son," I understood why Pereira risks paying him for articles he knows cannot be published because of their implicit critique of Portugal's authoritarian regime.

I have never agreed with the claim that art must be kept separate from politics. In *Pereira* I found the definitive rejection of that position. I was captivated by the protagonist's reluctant political awakening, by his final act of rebellion, so quiet and so reckless at the same time. Here was a novel with the courage to be a book about art, a book about politics, and a book about the politics of art—and the skill to achieve emotional resonances that were devastating.

When I returned to New York from San Francisco, I promptly began to recommend *Pereira* to everyone who asked me for the name of a great book to read.

It was not long before I went back to *Pereira* myself. I had just published my first novel earlier that year, and I had begun work on my second. I had consciously chosen to do something different this time, to abandon multiple narrators and essayistic interludes for an approach more restrained, seemingly simple—and brief. I had first encountered *Pereira* primarily as a reader. When I looked at it again, months later, I did so as an apprentice.

I began by trying to understand how *Pereira* managed to achieve so much with so few words. But I was soon asking myself another question. How, with such serious and pressing concerns, did *Pereira* manage to be so difficult to put down? Put differently, how could this most literary of novels also be such a thrilling page-turner?

I found my answers in *Pereira*'s form. *Pereira*'s brevity, it seemed to me, gave the novel a lightness that counterbalanced the weight of its subject matter. Moreover, because it was short it was able to move quickly, or at least able to give the impression of moving quickly. After all, there was only so much ground for the reader to cover between beginning and end.

But even though its compactness was unusual, what seemed to me most striking about the form of *Pereira* was its use of the testimonial. The novel is not a traditional third-person narrative in which Pereira is himself merely a character. Nor is it a traditional first-person narrative in which Pereira tells us the story of his "I." Instead we have a testimony, with Pereira presumably testifying to an account of his actions transcribed by someone else.

The result is mysterious, menacing, enthralling, and mind-bending—all at once. Through the testimonial form, Pereira makes detectives of its readers. We are unsettled and given more to do. An unexpected interpretative space opens up before us, nags at us, seduces us. We feel more like characters than we are used to. And if my experience is anything to go by, we love it.

Pereira's politics grow more pressing by the day, as absolutist ideologies and paranoid states increasingly impact our lives. And the lessons *Pereira* teaches about how fiction works have the power to transform. Certainly they changed this writer. Without *Pereira*, my own second novel would not have been written as it is. For that, and for the pleasure *Pereira* has repeatedly given me, I am deeply grateful.

(2010)

My Reluctant Fundamentalist

IN THE SUMMER OF 2000, I began writing my second novel. I was living on Cornelia Street in New York's West Village, working as a management consultant at McKinsey & Company with the unusual understanding that I would be allowed to disappear from the office for three months a year to write. I was close to paying off the hundred thousand dollars in loans I had taken out to finance law school; I had published my first novel, *Moth Smoke*, a few months earlier; and I was able to return regularly for extended periods to Lahore, the city in Pakistan where I had mostly grown up. The time had come for me to decide what to do with my life, and where to do it.

The choices I faced were confusing. New York or Lahore? Novelist as my entire profession or as only a part? And the choices were related. If I left my job to write full-time, I would lose my employment-based work visa and be forced to depart permanently for Pakistan. As I had done once before, I turned to my writing to help me understand my split self and my split world. *Moth Smoke* had for me been a look at Pakistan with a gaze altered by the many years I had spent in America. *The Reluctant Fundamentalist*, I thought, would be a look at America with a gaze reflecting the part of myself that remained stubbornly Pakistani.

By the summer of 2001 I had produced a draft. I had consciously moved away from the multiple first-person narration and freestyle riffs of *Moth Smoke*. I had instead written a stripped-down, utterly minimalist love story of a young Pakistani man in New York who is troubled by the notion that he is a modern-day janissary serving the empire of American corporatism. The style was that of a fable, of a parable, the kind of folk or religious story one looks to for guidance, because of course guidance was what I needed.

But upon reading it my agent told me he was puzzled by the protagonist's inner conflict: why would so secular and Westernized a Muslim man feel such tension with America? I told him there was deep resentment in much of the rest of the world toward the sole remaining superpower, and I resigned myself to a process of writing that would mirror that of my first novel, which took some seven drafts and seven years to complete. I also accepted a temporary transfer to my firm's London office as a way of deferring my life decisions, thinking the city lay geographically and culturally midway between New York and Lahore. And so it was from across the Atlantic in September that I watched the World Trade Center fall in a place I still thought of as home.

The rest of that year was one of great turmoil for me. Muslim friends of mine in America began to be questioned and harassed; I was distressed by the war in Afghanistan; traveling on my Pakistani passport became increasingly unpleasant; and then, following the December terrorist attacks on India's parliament, it looked as though India might invade Pakistan. Lahore sits on the border, just a few miles from what would have been the front line. I knew I needed to be there with my family. So I took a leave of absence and went back, moving into my old room.

That crisis eventually passed. But my novel made little progress. I had chosen to keep it set in the year before September 11, so that my characters would not be overwhelmed by an event that spoke so much more loudly than any individual's story could. I grew personally more divided, saddened and dismayed by the heavy-handedness of the Bush administration's conduct abroad. I decided to make my transfer to London permanent. I met the woman I would later marry when she was visiting the city on holiday. I was inspired to quit my job. Until she moved to London after our wedding, I was often on airplanes between there and Lahore.

Eventually, I realized that, just as in my exterior world, there was no escaping the effects of September 11 in the interior world that was my novel. The story of a Pakistani man in New York who leaves just before that cataclysmic event would inevitably be bathed in the glare of the reader's knowledge of what would happen immediately after. I also felt enough time had passed for me to have something of the distance that distinguishes a novelist's perspective from a journalist's. So I rewrote the novel once again, this time set around the period of September 11, and I finished early in 2005.

The novel was still short, and the basic arc of the plot was unchanged. But I had chosen to shift the voice into an American-accented first person. My intention was to tell a story that felt, for the first third, deceptively familiar, a tale of the sort of American dream now so often told that it lulls us into a lazy complacency. Then, relying on the strength of that bond between reader and narrator, I would venture into more and more emotionally disturbing territory.

This did not entirely work, unfortunately, as my agent and a former editor made clear to me when they read it. But I could see I was close to something now. For me, writing a novel is like solving a puzzle. I had tried variations of minimalism in the third person, with voices ranging from fable to noir. I had tried the comforting oral cadences of an American-accented first person. But there was not enough of Pakistan in my novel, and it felt wrong somehow both to my ear, in its sound, and to my eye, in its architecture.

I was energized by this near miss, and I soon had my answers: the frame of a dramatic monologue in which the Pakistani protagonist speaks to an American listener, and a voice born of the British colonial inflections taught in elite Pakistani schools and colored by an anachronistic, courtly menace that resonates well with popular Western preconceptions of Islam.

Even as I wrote it I knew it would be the final draft. I was done a year later, in February 2006, and it sold almost immediately.

Writing now, in March 2007, as *The Reluctant Fundamentalist* is finally born, I feel its difficult gestation has helped me. I am still split between America and Pakistan. But I feel more comfortable with my relationship to both places than I have in a long time. People often ask me if I am the book's Pakistani protagonist. I wonder why they never ask if I am his American listener. After all, a novel can often be a divided man's conversation with himself.

(2007)

6

Rereading
—

Get Fit with Haruki
Murakami
—

Enduring Love of the
Second Person

Rereading

I TEND TO REREAD small books. This wasn't always the case—when I was younger I reread long volumes, too. I spent many a summer making my way, again and again, through Tolkien's capacious fantasies and Frank Herbert's sprawling sci-fi. But in the two decades that I have been writing novels myself I have reread infrequently, and what I have reread has mostly been short. Tabucchi's *Pereira Declares* tugs me back now, and Murakami's *Sputnik Sweetheart*. Perhaps it is because I find the slender literary long form innately interesting. Perhaps it is because novels are like affairs, and small novels—with fewer pages of plot to them—are affairs with less history, affairs that involved just a few glances across a dinner table or a single ride together, unspeaking, on a train, and therefore affairs still electric with potential, still heart-quickening, even after the passage of all these years.

(2012)

Get Fit with Haruki Murakami

WHEN I MOVED back to Lahore a few years ago, I left my writer friends behind. I had cousins in Lahore, a couple dozen of them, and tight childhood buddies, and aunts and uncles and nephews and nieces. But no writers I was really close to, not at first. No one I could meet for a drink to talk shop. For that, I still needed to visit my former hometowns of New York and London, which didn't happen more than a couple of times a year.

I was happy to be away from the noise of publishing: the book launches, the award ceremonies, the cycle of who got reviewed how this week. But I missed the camaraderie. Novel writing is solitary work. In Lahore it became a solitary profession, too.

So I started reading novelists to hang out with them. Not their novels, which of course I'd always read, but their memoirs, their essays on their writing, their interviews. I dug out old classics like *A Moveable Feast*. I asked my neighborhood bookshop to order up Márquez on Márquez, Calvino on Calvino, the multiple volumes of the *Paris Review* Interviews. Ah, the *Paris Review* Interviews: orgiastic to a writer who's been on his own awhile, let me tell you.

It was in volume 4 that I came across one with Haruki Murakami, a writer I'd long admired. And halfway into that interview, I found this quote, which I wound up rereading so often that I copied it out and taped it to my printer: "Writing a long novel is like survival training. Physical strength is as necessary as artistic sensitivity."

I liked this. Not that I thought it was true. But I liked it. Yes, Tolstoy did his share of war fighting, and Hemingway was a tough guy. But I'm not sure Nabokov could bench his weight. And I had the sense Virginia Woolf couldn't, either (although her biographical details were sketchy in my mind; maybe Bloomsbury was the Octagon of its era).

Nonetheless, like much else that comes from Murakami, that quote only seems easily dismissed while managing somehow to stick with you. There's a fine line between "you've got to be kidding" and genius, and Murakami walks it all the time. Or runs it, as it turns out. Because I next bought his memoir-cum-musings-on-writing, *What I Talk About When I Talk About Running*, and learned the man runs like a fiend. He runs miles a day, every day. And then sometimes he swims. He's done ultra-marathons, triathlons. He doesn't just talk the talk. He splashes-runs-pedals the hell out of the walk.

Now, at the time I encountered the Murakami quote, I was

stuck. My third novel was going nowhere. Maybe it was being a new father. Maybe it was the spate of terrorist bombings hitting Lahore. Maybe it was the heat—and the cold, because although Lahore is mostly warm, the short winters can get pretty cold and natural gas shortages plus poor insulation mean you're cold indoors, constantly. But probably it was none of those things. My first two novels took seven years each, and I throw out draft after draft. Being stuck comes as naturally to me as running comes to Murakami.

I needed to get unstuck. And, nearing the age of forty, I'd already used up many of the usual tricks writers before me had employed to shake things up when they were in a rut: travel chemically, break your heart, change continents, get married, have a child, quit your job, etc. I was desperate. So I started to walk. Every morning. First thing, as soon as I got up, which as a dad now meant six or seven a.m. I walked for half an hour. Then I walked for an hour. Then I walked for ninety minutes. My wife was amused. Good-bye Hamid, hello Hamster—that sort of thing.

(As an aside, a cousin of mine in Karachi, an anti-intellectual, hard-partying, gun-carrying, off-for-the-weekend-in-his-jeep-hunting kind of guy, took up reading around this time. His wife would wake to find him with the night-light on, engrossed in a novel. "It's weird," she told him, "but I like it." She called it his midlife crisis.)

Murakami's quote is about writing long novels. I write short novels. So it made sense that while he has to run to get fit enough to do what he has to do, I could manage with just walking. And, the significant speed difference notwithstanding, a daily five-mile walk turned out to be exactly what I needed. My head cleared. My energy soared. My neck pains diminished. Sometimes I texted myself ideas, sentences, entire paragraphs as I walked. Other times I just floated along, arms at my sides, stewing and filtering and looking.

Walking unlocked me. It's like LSD. Or a library. It does things to you. I finished my novel in only two more years (for a total of six), walking every day. And I don't plan on stopping. If the choice is between extended periods of abject writing failure and prescription orthotics, I know which side my man Murakami and I are on.

I'm now gearing up to launch into novel four. Murakami's quote is still taped to my printer. It's been joined by a cluster of others: senior writers I haven't met, helping out a frequently struggling younger colleague in Lahore.

They collectively surround, I've just noticed, an old piece of paper. It's a to-do list I've been ignoring, and should really take care of.

(2013)

Enduring Love of the
Second Person

I THINK I'VE ALWAYS been drawn to the second person. When I was growing up and playing with my friends, the usual way we interacted with imaginary worlds was as characters: a bench was "your" boat, leaves on a lawn were the fins of sharks out to get "you." Make-believe storytelling, which is to say fiction, wasn't exclusively about being an observer—not for me, at least. There was this other strand as well, of being a participant.

Just before my family moved back to Pakistan, I encountered Dungeons & Dragons as a nine-year-old in California. That fantasy game was spellbinding for me. To understand the rules, you had to read books. But then you were free to create. It was collective imagining with a shared narrative. The Dungeon Master—a figure somewhere between an author and a referee—set in motion a tale that players spun together. It was as a DM, I'm pretty sure, that my proto-novelistic skills were first honed.

Of course, I read a lot, too. There seemed to be a constant stream of asides directly addressing the reader in children's books, a sort of conspiratorial "you" that cropped up again and again. Then there were those hybrids of role-playing game and children's book: game books like the Choose Your Own Adventure series, which briefly, in that time before computers were readily available, occupied a full shelf of my neighborhood bookshop in Lahore.

Slowly, from comic books and sci-fi and sword and sorcery, my reading interests stretched out in my late teens to encompass Hemingway and Tolstoy and Márquez. When I moved back to America for college and signed up for a creative writing class, I had no idea I wanted to be a writer. When the semester ended, I didn't want to be anything else.

In my final year, as I was starting my first novel, I read *The Fall* by Camus. It is written as a dramatic monologue, with the protagonist constantly addressing the reader as "you," and it changed how I thought books could work. I was amazed by the potential of the "you," of how much space it could open up in fiction.

The book I was writing then, back in 1993, became *Moth Smoke*, the tale of a pot-smoking ex-banker who falls disastrously in love with his best friend's wife. You, the reader, are cast as his judge. The story has what might be called a realistic narrative—there is no magic, no aliens—but the frame of the trial that it uses isn't realism. It is something else: make-believe, play, with "you" given an active role.

In my second novel, *The Reluctant Fundamentalist*, I wanted to explore this further, push the boundaries of what I knew how to do with "you." Camus's novel was a guide, but my project was my own: to try to show, after the terrorist attacks of 9/11, how feelings already present inside a reader—fear, anger, suspicion, loyalty—could color a narrative so that the reader, as much as or even more than the writer, is deciding what is really going on. I wanted the novel to be a kind of mirror, to let readers see how they are reading, and, therefore, how they are living and how they are deciding their politics.

By the time I started work on my third book, I'd come to believe that novels weren't passive forms of entertainment. Novels were a way for readers to create, not just for writers to do so. Novels were different from, say, film and television, because readers got more of the source code—the abstract symbols we call letters and words—and assembled more of the story themselves. Novels didn't come with sound tracks or casting directors.

I thought my next novel should try to be explicit about this, about the nature of the reader-writer relationship, the notion that "you" could simultaneously be audience and character and maker. My growing sense was that a kind of self-expression (and self-transcendence, and even self-help) is central to what fiction does, both for writers and for readers. And so *How to Get Filthy Rich in Rising Asia* was born, a novel that is a self-help book that is a second-person life story that is an invitation to create. Together.

We're born with an in-built capacity for language. It is wired into our brains, just as an in-built capacity for breathing is wired into our lungs. We need language. We need language to tell stories. We need stories to create a self. We need a self because the complexity of the chemical processes that make up our individual humanities exceeds the processing power of our brains.

The self we create is a fiction. On this point, religion and cognitive neuroscience converge. When the machine of a human being is turned on, it seems to produce a protagonist, just as a television produces an image. I think this protagonist, this self, often recognizes that it is a fictional construct, but it also recognizes that thinking of itself as such might cause it to disintegrate.

Maybe, therefore, it prefers to encounter itself obliquely. Maybe our selves are more comfortable exploring their fictional natures in stories that are themselves avowedly fictional—in novels, for example. Maybe novels are where our selves get to put up their feet, take off their clothes and makeup and dentures, cut loose with an echoing fart, and be a little truer to what they are for a bit, before they are once more pressed into service, sealed in their uniforms, and dispatched to face a reality in which they can't, for good reason, entirely believe.

(2013)

7

Are We Too Concerned That
Characters Be "Likable"?

Where Is the Great American
Novel by a Woman?

How Do E-Books Change the
Reading Experience?

Are the New "Golden Age"
TV Shows the New
Novels?

Are We Too Concerned That Characters Be "Likable"?

FOR MOST OF my life, I can't remember having thought much about whether fictional characters were likable. But when I was visiting New York recently, my editor of fifteen years told me she liked to go to the website of a leading Internet retailer, as well as to the site of a formerly independent book community, since acquired by that retailer, and see what readers had to say about the books she published. One of the things readers discussed a great deal, she said, was whether characters were likable—nonlikability being, in the minds of many, a serious flaw.

How interesting, I thought then. How different from how I read. But I've been reconsidering the matter. And, on reflection, maybe I shouldn't have been so surprised.

I'll confess—I read fiction to fall in love. That's what's kept me hooked all these years. Often, that love was for a character: in a presexual-crush way for Fern in *Charlotte's Web*; in a best-buddies way for the heroes of *Astérix & Obélix*; in a sighing, "I wish there were more of her in this book" way for Jessica in *Dune* or Arwen in *The Lord of the Rings*.

In fiction, as in my nonreading life, someone didn't necessarily have to be likable to be lovable. Was Anna Karenina likable? Maybe not. Did part of me fall in love with her when I cracked open a secondhand hardcover of Tolstoy's novel, purchased in a bookshop in Princeton, New Jersey, the day before I headed home to Pakistan for a hot, slow summer? Absolutely.

What about Humbert Humbert? A pedophile. A snob. A dangerous madman. The main character of Nabokov's *Lolita* wasn't very likable. But that voice. Ah. That voice had me at "fire of my loins."

So I discovered I could fall in love with a voice. And I could fall in love with form, with the dramatic monologue of Camus's *The Fall*, or, more recently, the first-person plural of Julie Otsuka's *The Buddha in the Attic*, or the restless, centerless perspective of Jennifer Egan's *A Visit from the Goon Squad*. And I'd always been able to fall in love with plot, with the story of a story.

Is all this the same as saying I fall in love with writers through their writing? I don't think so, even though I do use the term that way. I'll say I love Morrison, I love Oates. Both are former teachers of mine, so they're writers I've met off the page. But still, what I mean is I love their writing. Or something about their writing.

Among the quotes I keep taped to the printer on my writing desk is this one, from Italo Calvino's *Invisible Cities*:

The inferno of the living is not something that will be; if there is one, it is what is already here, the inferno where we live every day, that we form by being together. There are two ways to escape suffering it. The first is easy for many: accept the inferno and become such a part of it that you can no longer see it. The second is risky and demands constant vigilance and apprehension: seek and learn to recognize who and what, in the midst of the inferno, are not inferno, then make them endure, give them space.

I wonder if reading, for me, is an attempt to recognize who and what are not inferno, and if the love I sometimes feel is the glimmer of this recognition.

I wonder if that is the case for many of us. Perhaps, in the widespread longing for likable characters, there is this: a desire, through fiction, for contact with what we've armored ourselves against in the rest of our lives, a desire to be reminded that it's possible to open our eyes, to see, to recognize our solitude—and at the same time to not be entirely alone.

(2013)

Where Is the Great American Novel by a Woman?

WHERE IS THE Great American Novel by a woman? Well, have a look at your bookshelf.

What else are those mind-blowing late-twentieth-century works by such American women as, among others, Kingston and Kingsolver, Morrison and Robinson, L'Engle and Le Guin, if not great novels? And in our own still-young twenty-first century, much of the most interesting American writing I, at least, happen to read seems to be coming from women, including Jennifer Egan, Julie Otsuka, A.M. Homes, and Karen Russell. (Nor is this a United States–specific phenomenon: over in Britain, where I served as a judge for this year's BBC National Short Story Award, we found ourselves announcing an all-women shortlist.)

Ah, I've heard it said too often, those woman-written books may be fine, there may be some good American novels among them, even great American novels, but they aren't the

Great American Novel. So I've come to make an announcement. There is no such thing.

The point of there being a notion of the Great American Novel is to elevate fiction. It's a target for writers to aim at. It's a mythological beast, an impossible mountaintop, a magical vale in the forest, a place to get storytellers dreaming of one day reaching. It keeps you warm when times are cold, and times in the world of writing for a living are mostly cold.

But if the idea of the Great American Novel is blinding us to exquisite fiction written by women, then perhaps its harm is exceeding its usefulness. Attempt, therefore, to resist the admittedly rich resonances that attach to the fact that a Muslim-named man who lives in Pakistan is performing this task, and bear with me as I advocate the death of the Great American Novel.

The problem is in the phrase itself. "Great" and "Novel" are fine. But "the" is needlessly exclusionary, and "American" is unfortunately parochial. The whole, capitalized, seems to speak to a deep and abiding insecurity, perhaps a colonial legacy. How odd it would be to call Homer's *Iliad* or Rumi's *Masnavi* "the Great Eastern Mediterranean Poem."

Elevated fiction reaches for transcendence. *Gatsby*'s beauty, *Blood Meridian*'s beauty, *Beloved*'s beauty don't lie in their capturing something quintessentially American, for there is no such thing. These novels reveal an America too vast and diverse to support unitary narratives. They split atoms to reveal

galaxies. Their beauties lie in attaining wisdom and crafts-
manship so exalted as to exceed our petty nationalisms—so
exalted, in other words, as to be human.

This wisdom may come from Americans and be set in
America, but it is bigger than notions of black or white, male
or female, American or non-. Human beings don't necessarily
exist inside of (or correspond to) the neat racial, gendered, or
national boxes into which we often unthinkingly place them.

It's a mistake to ask literature to reinforce such structures.
Literature tends to crack them. Literature is where we free
ourselves. Otherwise, why imagine at all? So drop the caps.
Drop the "the." Drop the "American." Unless you think you're
working on the Great American Novel. In which case, if it
helps, keep the notion of it alive in your heart, no longer as a
target to hit, but as the gravity you must defy to break from
orbit and soar into space.

We're out here. Waiting for you. Foreigners. Freaks, every
last one. Your laws call us aliens. But you know better. You've
grappled with the freakiness within. You're part of us. And we
of you.

Welcome, American. Now tell us about Topeka. Or Tai-
wan. And, by the way, have you brought along a copy of the
latest Oates?

(2013)

How Do E-Books Change the Reading Experience?

THE ADVANTAGES OF e-books are clear. E-books are immediate. Sitting at home in Pakistan, I can read an intriguing review of a book, one not yet in stores here, and with the click of a button be reading that book in an instant. E-books are also incorporeal. While traveling, which I do frequently, I can bring along several volumes, weightless and indeed without volume, thereby enabling me to pack only a carry-on bag.

And yet the experience of reading e-books is not always satisfactory. Yes, it is possible to vary the size of the font, newly important to me at age forty-two, as I begin to perceive my eye muscles weakening. Yes, e-books can be read in the dark, self-illuminated, a convenient feature when my wife is asleep and I am too lazy to leave our bed, or when electricity outages in Lahore have persisted for so long that our backup batteries are depleted. And yes, they offer more frequent indicators of progress, their click-forwards arriving at a rapidity that far exceeds that of paper flipping, because pixelated

screens tend to hold less data than printed pages and furthermore advance singly, not in two-sided pairs.

Nonetheless, often I prefer reading to e-reading. Or rather,
given that the dominance of paper can no longer be assumed,
p-reading to e-.

I think my reasons are related to the fact that I have
disabled the browser on my mobile phone. I haven't deleted it.
Instead, I've used the restrictions feature in my phone's operating system to hide the browser, requiring me to enter a code
to expose and enable it. I can use the browser when I find it
necessary to browse. But, for the most part, this setting serves
as a reminder to question manufactured desires, to resist unless I have good cause.

Similarly, I have switched my e-mail account from the
attention- and battery-consuming "push" setting to the less
frenzied manual one. E-mails are fetched when I want them to
be, which is not all that often. And the browser on my slender
fruit knife of a laptop now contains a readout that reminds (or
is it warns?) me how much time I have spent online.

Time is our most precious currency. So it's significant that
we are being encouraged, wherever possible, to think of our
attention not as expenditure but as consumption. This blurring of labor and entertainment forms the basis, for example,
of the financial alchemy that conjures deca-billion-dollar valu-
ations for social-networking companies.

I crave technology, connectivity. But I crave solitude, too.
As we enter the cyborg era, as we begin the physical shift to

human-machine hybrid, there will be those who embrace this epochal change, happily swapping cranial space for built-in processors. There will be others who reject the new ways entirely, perhaps even waging holy war against them, with little chance—in the face of drones that operate autonomously while unconcerned shareholding populations post selfies and status updates—of success. And there will be people like me, with our powered exoskeletons left often in the closet, able to leap over buildings when the mood strikes us, but also prone to wandering naked and feeling the sand of a beach between our puny toes.

In a world of intrusive technology, we must engage in a kind of struggle if we wish to sustain moments of solitude. E-reading opens the door to distraction. It invites connectivity and clicking and purchasing. The closed network of a printed book, on the other hand, seems to offer greater serenity. It harks back to a pre-jacked-in age. Cloth, paper, ink: for these read helmet, cuirass, shield. They afford a degree of protection and make possible a less intermediated, less fractured experience. They guard our aloneness. That is why I love them, and why I read printed books still.

(2014)

Are the New "Golden Age" TV Shows the New Novels?

MOVIES HAVE ALWAYS seemed to me a much tighter form of storytelling than novels, requiring greater compression, and in that sense falling somewhere between the short story and the novel in scale. To watch a feature film is to be immersed in its world for an hour and a half, or maybe two, or exceptionally three. A novel that takes only three hours to read would be a short novel indeed, and novels that last five times as long are commonplace.

Television is more capacious. Episode after episode, and season after season, a serial drama can uncoil for dozens of hours before reaching its end. Along the way, its characters and plot have room to develop, to change course, to congeal. In its near limitlessness, TV rivals the novel.

What once sheltered the novel were differences in the quality of writing. Films could be well written, but they were smaller than novels. TV was big, but its writing was clunky. The novel had *Pride and Prejudice*; TV had *Dynasty*. But television has made enormous leaps in the last decade or so. The writing has improved remarkably, as have the acting, direction, and design.

Recently we've been treated to many shows that seem better than any that came before: the brilliant ethnography of *The Wire*, the dazzling sci-fi of *Battlestar Galactica*, the gorgeous period re-creation of *Mad Men*, the gripping fantasy of *Game of Thrones*, the lacerating self-exploration of *Girls*. Nor is TV's rise confined to shows originating in only one country. Pakistani, Indian, British, and dubbed Turkish dramas are all being devoured here in Pakistan. Thanks to downloads, even Denmark's *Borgen* has found its local niche.

I now watch a lot of TV. And I'm not alone, even among my colleagues. Ask novelists today whether they spend more time watching TV or reading fiction and prepare yourself, at least occasionally, to hear them say the unsayable.

That this represents a crisis for the novel seems to me undeniable. But a crisis can be an opportunity. It incites change. And the novel needs to keep changing if it is to remain novel. It must, pilfering a phrase from TV, boldly go where no one has gone before.

In the words of the Canadian writer Sheila Heti: "Now that there are these impeccable serial dramas, writers of fiction should feel let off the hook more—not feel obliged to worry so much about plot or character, since audiences can get their fill of plot and character and story there, so novelists can take off in other directions, like what happened with painting when photography came into being more than a hundred years ago. After that there was an incredible flourishing of the art, in so many fascinating directions. The novel should only do what the serial drama could never do."

Television is not the new novel. Television is the old novel.

In the future, novelists need not abandon plot and character, but would do well to bear in mind the novel's weirdness. At this point in our technological evolution, to read a novel is to engage in probably the second-largest single act of pleasure-based data transfer that can take place between two human beings, exceeded only by sex. Novels are characterized by their intimacy, which is extreme, by their scale, which is vast, and by their form, which is linguistic and synesthetic. The novel is a kinky beast.

Television gives us something that looks like a small world, made by a group of people who are themselves a small world. The novel gives us sounds pinned down by hieroglyphs, refracted flickerings inside an individual.

Sufis tell of two paths to transcendence: one is to look out at the universe and see yourself, the other is to look within yourself and see the universe. Their destinations may converge, but television and the novel travel in opposite directions.

(2014)

POLITICS

8

The Usual Ally

—

Divided We Fall

—

After Sixty Years, Will
   Pakistan Be Reborn?

The Usual Ally

I REMEMBER, as a boy in Lahore, the moment I learned
Pakistan had become, once again, America's ally. I was
with my cousin in front of my grandfather's house. It had been
raining, and water stood an inch deep on the lawn. Armed
with three bricks, the two of us were battling nature. I would
put a brick down and move onto it, my cousin would step onto
the one I had left, and then he would hand forward the brick
he had been standing on a moment before. We were most of
the way across when my mother told us to come in. The adults
were watching the news. I was told we were now allied with
America against the Soviets in Afghanistan. Cool, I thought.
We were with the good guys and we would win. I had seen
enough cartoons and films to have no doubt about it.

The war went on for the rest of my childhood, but it was
mainly a distant, faraway thing. Still, as I got older I began to
realize that odd things were going on. Our dictator was giving
speeches about transforming Pakistan into a society based on

his interpretation of Islam. Painted images of F-16s given by America were appearing on the backs of buses under the words "God is great." Armed college students were telling women to cover their heads.

I went to college in America soon after the Soviets were defeated. Surprisingly, few Americans I met seemed to think of Pakistan as an ally. Fewer still knew where Pakistan was. After the war, America turned its back. Aid and military supplies were cut off. My friends at home were shocked by this. I, living in America, was less surprised. In America, the murky, unknown places of the world are blank screens: stories of evil can be projected on them with as little difficulty as stories of good.

Now Pakistan is once again dragged into the front line. There was already tension in Pakistan between the graduates of religious madrassas and those of state and private schools. But since the last Afghan war, Pakistan has been struggling toward a compromise between these groups. Such compromises evolve slowly, and are nourished by stability. In acting now, Americans must consider the consequences of projecting a war film onto what is not a blank screen at all. They must have compassion as they weigh the impact of polarizing millions of people in the name of justice. In Pakistan, my friends and family are frightened, as they should be when the most powerful military in the world is sent to do a task best accomplished by schoolteachers, police forces, persuasion, and time.

(2001)

Divided We Fall

W HEN I MADE a reporting trip to Pakistan's rugged Balochistan province in 2004, I expected to encounter strong feelings against the central government in Islamabad. Balochistan was in the grip of a low-level insurgency, with tribesmen demanding greater autonomy for the province. Just days before my trip, a roadside bomb in the Baloch fishing village of Gwadar had killed five Chinese engineers working on Pakistan's premier development project: a massive new port. So I was surprised to see children in Gwadar playing cricket in replicas of the uniforms of Pakistan's national team. In fact, the only hostility I encountered was from aggressive undercover security agents who questioned me rudely and threatened to seize my camera.

Afterward, a shop owner, overhearing me complain on the phone about my treatment, invited me to his home for lunch. "The army is disrespectful to us," he said. "They take away our young men and beat them for no reason. We are Pakistanis, but they treat us like foreigners." And so, in his opinion, did the central government. "None of the work on the port has gone to people from Gwadar," he added. "They are spending billions of rupees on it, but they have not even built us a proper hospital." Like the children playing cricket, he seemed to consider himself very much a Pakistani. But he resented Islamabad's heavy-handed approach and the troops it deployed to enforce its policies. I left Gwadar with new sympathy for the Baloch and their desire for more say in their affairs.

Two years later, the insurgency in Balochistan has grown. And last week's announcement by the army that it has killed Nawab Akbar Khan Bugti is a sign that the military has failed to understand that its belligerent tactics only make matters worse. Bugti was a rebel leader and a member of an oppressive class of tribal chieftains who control much of Balochistan as their personal fiefdom. But he was also a former governor of the province and a respected elder to many Baloch. His death, which has triggered unrest and rioting in Balochistan, is symbolic of our government's refusal to address the grievances of large numbers of Pakistanis who feel ignored and marginalized by Islamabad's policies. Most Baloch, for example, believe they do not receive a fair share of the revenues from the natural gas produced in their province.

I was originally opposed to the 1999 coup that brought the president, General Pervez Musharraf, to power. But after 9/11 and the war against the Taliban in Afghanistan, he seemed to offer a steady and in some ways liberal hand during a period of great uncertainty for Pakistan. Under Musharraf, we have witnessed rapid economic growth and a soaring stock market, a liberalization of private media outlets, and the resumption of a peace process with India. But that sense of hope is now fading. One of the legacies of seven years of rule by the army chief is a Pakistan that has become deeply divided.

The fissures are visible at multiple levels. The most obvious example is that of attack helicopters hunting down rebels in Balochistan and the tribal areas of our northwest frontier— rebels who are our fellow citizens. But equally dangerous is the chronic failure of our provinces to agree on new dams essential to meeting our future needs for water. Or the inability of our society to channel dissent into debate, an inability that means the publication of cartoons in a newspaper in Denmark is able to provoke not just a response in our own newspapers, but also riots that transform our cities into virtual battlegrounds. The failure to bridge such divisions is particularly dangerous for Pakistan as a country with myriad ethnic and religious groups. The rich-poor divide feeds the waves of crime rocking cities like Karachi, and the ideological war between Sunni and Shia Muslims fuels domestic terrorism.

What Pakistan needs is compromise: between provinces, between religion and secularism, between the desire for growth and the imperative to check inflation, between us and our neighbors. But a government led by a president in a soldier's uniform has proven ill-suited to striking compromises. So we must try the alternative: a return to democracy, with its inherent horse trading, messiness, and false starts. Such a transition will not be without risk, and many Pakistanis are frightened by the potential for instability. But the alternative, a continuation of the status quo, in which our president lacks the legitimacy that comes from having stood in a fair election and large segments of the country feel unrepresented by the state, is even riskier.

The first challenge, of course, is to convince Musharraf to stand down at the end of his current term and allow the elections scheduled for 2007 to be free and fair. He would do well to bear in mind that the people of Gwadar want jobs and a hospital, not army checkpoints. No matter how many tribal chiefs are killed, in this the people of Gwadar will never be alone.

(2006)

After Sixty Years, Will Pakistan Be Reborn?

SIXTY YEARS AGO, British India was granted independence and partitioned into Hindu-majority India and my native nation, Muslim-majority Pakistan. It was a birth of exceptional pain.

Handed down to me through the generations is the story of my namesake, my Kashmir-born great-grandfather. He was stabbed by a Muslim as he went for his daily stroll in Lahore's Lawrence Gardens. Independence was only a few months away, and the communal violence that would accompany the partition was beginning to simmer.

My great-grandfather was attacked because he was mistaken for a Hindu. This was not surprising; as a lawyer, most of his colleagues were Hindus, as were many of his friends. He would shelter some of their families in his home during the murderous riots that were to come.

But my great-grandfather was a Muslim. More than that, he was a member of the Muslim League, which had campaigned for the creation of Pakistan. From the start, Pakistan has been prone to turning its knife upon itself.

Yet 1947 is also remembered in my family as a time of enormous hope. My great-grandfather survived. And the birth that year of his grandson, my father, marked the arrival of a first generation of something new: Pakistanis.

My mother recalls a childhood of sugar and flour rations. The 1950s, she says, were a decade of a young country finding its feet. She grew up in a small town and she describes a fierce love for Pakistan felt by her and her schoolmates. Pakistan was theirs, a source of pride and identity, symbolically both a parent and, because it inspired such feelings of protectiveness, a sibling.

In the 1960s, my mother's family moved to Lahore, which had been the cultural and governmental center of Punjab Province before the region was ripped apart at independence. By then, Pakistan's economy had begun to boom. My parents speak of cinemas showing the latest films, colleges producing idealistic graduates, and young couples walking along the banks of the River Ravi.

Yet Pakistan's true glory at that time was the southern port of Karachi, where my uncle, then a young banker, went to live. It was, he says, a vibrant and cosmopolitan city, a place of cafés and sea breezes and visiting international flight crews; it hummed with the energy and ingenuity of millions of former refugees who had come from India.

Still, these rosy family recollections paint an incomplete

picture. For the civilian government of Pakistan had been deposed by a military coup in 1958. General Muhammad Ayub Khan was a steadfast American ally against the Soviet Union and the recipient of large amounts of American weaponry and aid.

But deprived of democracy for much of my parents' youth, Pakistanis were unable to articulate an inclusive vision of what their country stood for. Making things worse, the country was divided in two, separated geographically by India. West Pakistan, the army's heartland, received far more than its fair share of resources. After years of mistreatment and rigged elections, East Pakistanis fought a war of independence, India took up arms on their side, and East Pakistan became the nation of Bangladesh.

I was born in 1971, the year of this second partition, as Pakistan once again turned its knife upon itself.

After the bloodshed, what was left of Pakistan was forced to ask what it stood for. Democracy was restored, and Prime Minister Zulfikar Ali Bhutto became wildly popular with a simple slogan: "Bread, clothing and a home." In other words, Pakistan existed to lessen the poverty of its citizens.

Bhutto was deposed in 1977 and hanged. So, like my parents before me, I was born in a democratic Pakistan but spent much of my youth in a dictatorship. And like General Ayub before him, the new dictator, General Muhammad Zia-ul-Haq, was a steadfast American ally against the Soviet Union. But whereas General Ayub had been largely secular, General

Zia envisioned Pakistan as a theocratic Muslim state. It became a staging ground for the anti-Soviet jihad in Afghanistan and underwent a dramatic process of social engineering called Islamization.

Although we disliked our president, my friends and I remained fiercely patriotic. We idolized Pakistani sporting heroes in cricket, field hockey, and squash. We felt a thrill of achievement when we listened to bootleg cassettes of the first Pakistani rock bands. For us, the success of anything Pakistani was a source of personal pride.

In 1988, shortly before I left for college in America, General Zia died in a suspicious airplane crash and civilian rule was again restored. But the democracy of the '90s was a disappointment, with power alternating between ineffective, feuding governments.

As my friends married and had children, a third generation of Pakistanis began to arrive. Like my parents' generation, and like mine, these children were born in a democracy but would spend their youth under pro-American military rule, this time under General Pervez Musharraf.

And now Pakistan is once again turning its knife on itself. Insurgencies simmer in the regions bordering Afghanistan, and suicide bombers have begun to kill fellow Pakistanis with increasing frequency.

For me personally, the sixtieth anniversary of independence, while worthy of note, is not of the utmost importance.

My hopes are already dashing ahead and attaching themselves to the elections that are scheduled for later this year.

On one side are the forces of exclusion, who wish Pakistan to stand only for their kind of Pakistani. These include the political descendants of the man who stabbed my great-grandfather, the people who seek to oppress those who are clean shaven or those who toil for meager wages or those who are from provinces other than their own. But arrayed against them is something wholly new.

Pakistan now has private television stations that refuse to let the government set the news agenda. It has a Supreme Court that has asserted its independence for the first time, restoring a chief justice suspended by the president. And it has an army under physical attack from within and in desperate need of compromise with civil society.

A sixtieth birthday brings with it the obligation to shed some illusions. Pakistanis must realize that we have been our own worst enemies. My wish for our national anniversary is this: that we finally take the knife we have turned too often upon ourselves and place it firmly in its sheath.

(2007)

9

A Beginning

Fear and Silence

Feverish and Flooded,
    Pakistan Can Yet Thrive

A Beginning

IN CONSIDERING President Obama's speech in Cairo, it is worth bearing in mind a simple truth: no human being is only a Muslim and no human being is only an American. The people one might call Muslims, or Americans, are also women and men; mothers, fathers, daughters, and sons; lovers and doctors and writers and schoolteachers; poor and wealthy; politically engaged and apathetic; sure in their beliefs and utterly uncertain. They are, in other words, complex, multidimensional, unique, and ever changing. Look closely at the solid mass called Muslims and you will see a cloud of a billion individual atoms.

Religion and nationality are but two of the myriad dimensions along which our personal identities are constructed. As human beings, we realize that instinctively. When someone holds open a closing door so we can board an elevator, the component of their identity we value is not that they are Muslim, or American, but rather that they are compassionate. It is when we are frightened, and especially when our fears are played up and redirected and preyed upon, that we tend to reduce others to simplified (and artificial) mono-identities of religion or nationality or race.

President Obama's speech was a welcome attempt to diminish our fear of one another. He said that Muslims and Americans overlap in seven million Muslim-American citizens, in centuries of shared history, and indeed in President Obama's own family. He drew attention to similarities between the Muslim, Christian, and Jewish faiths. He stood up against crude stereotyping. He rejected the notion that Islam and the United States are in competition. He called for mutual respect, greater engagement, and more openness.

His speech was a promising beginning, a hopeful departure from the terrifying character of the previous United States administration. But in order for the speech to be more than a beginning, it will need to be followed by actions. As a novelist, I hold words in high regard, and I am grateful for many of the words I heard President Obama say. Such a dramatic change in tone can make deeds previously impossible possible. But those deeds will determine how President Obama's speech is judged by history.

There are reasons for optimism. The passage of the speech that has stayed with me most is: "The United States does not accept the legitimacy of continued Israeli settlements." It is becoming increasingly evident that President Obama intends to bring substantial pressure on Israel to reach a lasting peace with the Palestinians. Words such as these, coupled with actions, have the potential to improve the lives of millions.

Similarly, the withdrawal of American soldiers from Iraq, the closing of the detention camp at Guantánamo Bay, and the disavowal of the use of torture were all real promises of change, and they gave the speech added weight, even if they had of course already been announced.

But other passages of the speech, for example on democracy, seemed to run counter to President Obama's own actions. Saudi Arabia and Egypt, among America's closest allies in the region, are resolutely undemocratic nations. Similarly, to speak of "preventing a nuclear arms race in the Middle East" as something ignited by Iran, without mentioning Israel's deployment of nuclear weapons, was disingenuous.

It is in these lapses that President Obama's challenge becomes clear. I think he is an exceptional man. I believe the world is fortunate to have him as president of the United States. But in the end, it is not possible to champion national greatness and human equality at the same time. Either the value placed on the life of an Iraqi or a Pakistani is equal to the value placed on the life of an American, or it is not. Either the value placed on the life of a Palestinian is equal to the value placed on the life of an Israeli, or it is not.

The United States needs to address this contradiction. It seeks to stand for national greatness and human equality. Yet its greatness is in part built upon the denial of the equality of others outside its borders. That denial stems from an emphasis being placed on one aspect of human identity, nationality, and it invites responses that similarly emphasize one aspect of human identity, such as religion.

Barack Hussein Obama has been elected president of the United States, not president of some world government. But his morality must be rooted primarily in his humanity, not in his office. His speech suggested that on the continuum between national greatness and human equality he stands closer to equality than did his predecessor. That is reason to celebrate. But I suspect most non-American Muslims, like most non-American non-Muslims, will hope that when President Obama said, "We do unto others as we would have them do unto us," he recognized the extraordinary magnitude of the shift in policies such a credo would require.

(2009)

Fear and Silence

WHY ARE AHMADIS persecuted so ferociously in Pakistan?

The reason can't be that their large numbers pose some sort of "threat from within." After all, Ahmadis are a relatively small minority in Pakistan. They make up somewhere between 0.25 percent (according to the last census) and 2.5 percent (according to *The Economist*) of our population.

Nor can the reason be that Ahmadis are non-Muslims. Pakistani Christians and Pakistani Hindus are non-Muslims, and similar in numbers to Pakistani Ahmadis. Yet Christians and Hindus, while undeniably discriminated against, face nothing like the vitriol directed toward Ahmadis in our country.

To understand what the persecution of Ahmadis achieves, we have to see how it works. Its first step is to say that Ahmadis are non-Muslims. And its second is to say that Ahmadis are not just non-Muslims but apostates: non-Muslims who claim to be Muslims while rejecting core tenets of Islam. These two steps are easy to take: any individual can choose to believe whatever they want about Ahmadis and their faith.

But the process goes further. Step three is to say that because Ahmadis are apostates, they should be victimized, or even killed. We are now beyond the realm of personal opinion. We are in the realm of group punishment and incitement to murder. Nor does it stop here. There is a fourth step. And step four is this: any Muslims who say Ahmadis should not be victimized or killed should themselves be victimized or killed.

In other words, even if they are not themselves Ahmadi, any policeman, doctor, politician, or passerby who tries to prevent, or just publicly opposes, the killing of an Ahmadi deserves to die. Why? Because people who defend apostates are apostates.

Aha.

This is what the persecution of Ahmadis achieves. It allows any Muslim to be declared an apostate. For the logic can be continued endlessly. When an Ahmadi man is wounded in an attack and goes to a hospital for treatment, if the doctor agrees to treat him, she is helping an apostate, and therefore she becomes an apostate and subject to threats. When a policeman is deputed to protect the doctor, since she is an apostate, the policeman is helping an apostate, so he, too, becomes an apostate. And on and on.

The collective result of this is to silence and impose fear not just on the tiny percentage of Pakistanis who are Ahmadis, or even on those who are Christians and Hindus, but on all of us. The message is clear. Speaking out against the problem means you become the problem, so you had better be quiet.

Our coerced silence is the weapon that has been sharpened and brought to our throats.

This is why Nawaz Sharif's statement in defense of Ahmadis met with such an angry response. Because the heart of the issue isn't whether Ahmadis are non-Muslims or not. The heart of the issue is whether Pakistanis can be silenced by fear.

Because if we can be silenced when it comes to Ahmadis, then we can be silenced when it comes to Shias, we can be silenced when it comes to women, we can be silenced when it comes to dress, we can be silenced when it comes to entertainment, and we can even be silenced when it comes to sitting by ourselves, alone in a room, afraid to think what we think.

That is the point.

(2010)

Feverish and Flooded, Pakistan Can Yet Thrive

L AST MONTH, it began to rain here in Lahore. It was my baby daughter's first monsoon. I took her out onto a balcony and held her as she stared blinkingly up at the dark sky. She was delighted. She laughed and kicked and reached for the drops shattering on her bare arms. The Pakistani monsoon is an amazing and beautiful thing.

The rains continued and, after particularly heavy downpours, the city's streets were transformed into temporary canals, cars either stalling or downshifting and revving their engines to pass. But Lahore drains quickly, and inconveniences in the city were for the most part brief. From elsewhere in the country, though, reports of crop damage and swollen rivers flooded in. The price of vegetables rose. Still the rains continued, and dikes that had held strong for decades gave way. The homes of many millions were ruined.

For me, to live in Pakistan is to know extremes of hope and despair. Hope takes many small forms. One of these is

Coke Studio, a televised jam session that throws together unexpected musical combinations, such as a soulful and powerfully voiced ex–fashion model accompanying a traditional male folk singer. It is part of a vast and downloadable music scene that circumvents the security concerns of live concerts through the use of mass media, the Internet and the country's one hundred million mobile phones. I have heard its songs as the ringtones of people ranging from bankers and shopkeepers to carpenters.

Countless individual responses to the floods also inspire hope. Massive collections are under way in Lahore. Virtually everyone I know is donating money, time, or goods—or all three—to the relief effort. Societal safety nets, the welfare micro-systems of families and friends that bind Pakistanis together in the absence of a strong and effective state, are doing what they can to help with the unprecedented load.

Hope also comes from the rise of a powerful and independent news media, and from a judiciary that has fought for—and won—remarkable freedom. Pakistan's airwaves and front pages, blogs, and cafés are full of the debates of a rambunctious multiparty democracy, one of precious few in the region between India and Europe.

Yet the battle against despair is a constant one. I feel it after each deadly terrorist attack, of which this year there have been half a dozen in Lahore alone, killing some two hundred people. I try not to think too much about the snipers on the rooftops of primary schools and the steel barricades at their gates, telling myself that my daughter still has some years left before she has to enroll.

It is difficult, however, to ignore the fact that the electricity to my house is cut off for a third of the day, Pakistan having failed to plan for rapidly growing demand. It is also difficult to ignore a general sense of malaise, of steadily dropping official standards, brought home recently by a tragic aircraft crash and multiple aviation near accidents in a single week.

And now there are the floods. The worst natural disaster in living memory, they have brought devastation to fourteen million Pakistanis, a number almost as large as the populations of New York and London combined. Pakistan normally ranks fourth in the world's production of cotton and milk, and tenth in wheat—but this terrible year it will not.

Slowly and painfully, however, Pakistan should recover. And beyond that, its future need not be bleak. The country's assets are enormous, after all. It has the world's sixth-largest population, with more children under the age of fourteen than the US. While poor, it has appreciably lower levels of hunger and child malnutrition than India.

Vitally, the country is building up its democratic institutions. This matters. For at its core, Pakistan suffers from two related ailments: a state doing too little for its people, and challengers seeking to supplant the state. Its fragile democracy holds the key to tackling both.

The first aspect of Pakistan's crisis can be boiled down to this: tax collection amounts to a paltry 10 percent of the country's gross domestic product. But the need to fund voters' expectations is creating pressures for change. If Pakistan is able to increase taxes as a proportion of GDP to India's 17 percent or Sri Lanka's 15 percent, the additional revenues would far exceed all foreign aid the country currently receives and make possible investments Pakistanis desperately need.

A more equitable and redistributive state would help, too, with the second aspect of Pakistan's crisis: attempts by militants to overthrow the government and subject the country's pluralistic and heterogeneous society to their tyrannical, intolerant writ.

But economic development is only part of the answer. The militants must also be fought, and the record thus far appears to be, unsurprisingly, that Pakistan's army is more effective at doing so when it operates under the umbrella of legitimacy conferred by a democratic government.

Yet the army has not, even now, committed fully to this fight, for it remains preoccupied with India. I believe this is a tragic mistake. But I also believe that it is unfair to say Pakistan should not feel threatened by its neighbor. I live thirty kilometers from a border where a million Indian soldiers recently massed in anger following an attack in the country by Pakistan-based militants. I have seen combat helicopters fly low overhead and artillery batteries dig into lawns. India and Pakistan's conflict is real, mutual, and nuclear-armed.

It must urgently be resolved. Pakistan's leading democratic parties appear eager to do so; the problem is security hawks on both sides. The world needs to lend a hand, shedding the pretense that no dispute over Kashmir exists—or that its consequences are minor. The truth is that Kashmir is a problem that destabilizes a region of 1.5 billion people and makes the planet more unsafe.

Recently, I met a Pakistani woman visiting Lahore from Hong Kong. Friends of hers abroad asked why she was traveling to such a troubled country. She said it was like visiting a loved one when they were sick. No one relishes exposing themselves to illness, but when a parent or sibling is unwell, human instinct is to be with them until they recover.

Pakistan is feverish these days. But I find much to admire and to keep me here, and I hope for the sake of my daughter's generation that one day soon the fever will break.

(2010)

10

Discontent and Its
   Civilizations

—

Uniting Pakistan's Minority
   and Majority

—

Osama bin Laden's Death

Discontent and Its Civilizations

R ECENTLY I WAS strolling along Amsterdam's canals with a pair of Pakistani immigrant friends. They were worried. The leader of the third-largest party in the Dutch Parliament had called for a ban on the Koran. Attitudes toward Muslims were becoming toxic. A strange thought hung over me as we wandered by marijuana-selling coffee shops and display windows for legal prostitutes: the thought that Anne Frank, as a permanent reminder of intolerance gone mad, could be a guardian angel for Muslims in Amsterdam. How sad that in this city, with its history, a religious minority could once again feel the need for such a guardian.

Suspicion of Muslims is, of course, not confined to Europe. Earlier this year, on a trip from Pakistan to New York with my wife and baby daughter, I had my usual lengthy encounter at JFK airport with an American version of the same theme. Sent to secondary inspection, I waited my turn to be investigated. Eventually it came, the officer questioning me about such things as whether I had ever been to Mexico or received combat training.

As a result, we were the last passengers on our flight to claim our luggage, a lonely set of suitcases and a foldable playpen on a now-stationary baggage carousel. And until we stepped out of the terminal, my heart kept pounding in a way incongruent with my status as a visitor with papers in order.

When we returned to Pakistan, a shock wave from a suicide bombing, the latest deadly attack by militants intent on destabilizing the country, passed through my sister's office in Lahore. The blast killed several people, but was far enough from the university where my sister teaches not to harm anyone on campus or shatter her windows. It did open her office door, though, pushing it firmly ajar, like a ghost exiting into the hallway outside.

Some might argue episodes such as these are signs of a clash of civilizations. But I think not. Individuals have commonalities that cut across different countries, religions, and languages—and differences that divide those who share a common country, religion, and language. The idea that we fall into civilizations, plural, is merely a politically convenient myth.

Take two notional civilizations, namely those of "Muslims" and "Westerners." To which do my Pakistani friends in Amsterdam or I belong? They are secular and believe in equal rights irrespective of gender or sexual orientation. And I, a citizen and resident of Pakistan, have spent seventeen years in America, longer than the lifetimes of more than seventy million Americans born since 1993.

Westernized Muslims, Islamized Westerners: surely people like us can be disregarded as recent, tiny, and unrepresentative minorities? Actually, no. Fly from Lahore to Madrid and you will find that the words for "shirt" and "soap" are virtually the same in both places, linguistic testament to the fact that people have always intermingled.

Yes, Pakistani murderers set off bombs that annually kill thousands. And yes, some Pakistanis fit the stereotype of poor, radicalized, seminary-educated militants. But they live in a nation where under 10 percent vote for parties of the religious right, where a rapidly growing majority watches television.

Pakistani television programming is incredibly diverse for good reason: so is the country. The blast wave that passed through my sister's office doubtless passed through devout Muslims, atheist Muslims, gay Muslims, funny Muslims, and lovestruck Muslims—not to mention Pakistani Christians, Chinese engineers, American security contractors, and Indian Sikhs. What civilization, then, did the bomb target? And from what civilization did it originate?

Civilizations are illusory. But they are useful illusions. They allow us to deny our common humanity, to allocate power, resources, and rights in ways repugnantly discriminatory.

To maintain the effectiveness of these illusions, they must

be associated with something undeniably real. That something is violence. Our civilizations do not cause us to clash. No, our clashing allows us to pretend we belong to civilizations.

In Pakistan, I live as part of an extended family. My parents built their house adjoining that of my grandparents. My wife and I built our apartment above the house of my parents. Our daughter needed a room. So we converted our balcony, adding a corrugated-metal, foam-insulated roof, and some well-shaded, double-glazed windows.

The room was bright, inexpensive, energy efficient, and quick to build. All we wanted, in other words. But then it occurred to us that our daughter's windows faced in the direction of a main road. A hundred yards away were offices, shops, banks. The kinds of places sometimes attacked in our city.

I decided to ask an architect friend whether I ought to consider blast-resistant film for my daughter's windows. Despite four generations of my family having lived in the same place, this was a question none of us had ever posed before. I had no idea whether such films were effective, or how much they might cost.

I did not wonder if they were made by factories in the West, by workers who were Muslim, by both, or by neither. No, I wondered instead if such films were truly transparent. For outside my daughter's windows is a yellow-blooming amaltas tree, beautiful and mighty, and much older than us all.

I hoped not to dim my daughter's view of it.

(2010)

Uniting Pakistan's Minority and Majority

THERE'S A NURSE I know in Lahore. She's tall and stocky, middle-aged. She is on call twenty-four hours a day and works six days a week. She's also a freelance head-hunter, placing cooks and drivers and maids. She sleeps little. She has five children to whom she hopes to give better lives. Last year, she donated time and money to flood victims.

She is a Pakistani Christian. And on Wednesday, I saw her weep.

She was staring at a TV set. It was reporting the assassination of Shahbaz Bhatti, Pakistan's federal minister for minorities, a Roman Catholic. "What's going to happen to Christians in this country?" she asked me.

I had no answer. But her question is searingly important. A country should be judged by how it treats its minorities. To the extent it protects them, it stands for the ennobling values of empathy and compassion, for justice rooted, not in might, but in human equality, and for civilization instead of savagery.

Pakistan ought to be exemplary in this regard. After all, ours is a nation of minorities: a patchwork of cultures, ethnicities, languages, and sects. Since independence, we've tried to use Islam to bind us together, to undo our inherent and pervasive minority-ness. After the country split in 1971, these appeals to religion expanded under Zulfikar Ali Bhutto and reached previously unimaginable extents under Zia-ul-Haq. They have continued to intensify ever since.

One problem with this approach, of course, has been that our religious minorities, a twentieth of our population, have been left out of our grand national narratives. Five percent may seem like a small proportion, but in absolute numbers it includes almost ten million Pakistanis, which equals everyone in Tunisia, or one and a half times all of Libya. If Pakistan's religious minorities were a country, they would be more populous than half the members of the UN.

So how have they been treated by Pakistan? Shamefully. They are looked down upon, discriminated against, physically threatened, and not infrequently killed. They are second-class citizens in every sense. Nor has our state offered them much support. Indeed, our state has been actively involved in their oppression.

None of this is new, of course. So, for those fortunate enough to belong to the religious majority, does it even matter?

Yes. Desperately. Minority relations are a microcosm of society. Each individual human being is, after all, a minority of one. And, as Pakistan becomes a country at war with its minorities, it is becoming a country at war with its individuals, with itself, with you and with me, with the human desire to be allowed to believe what we believe. In this direction lies Orwellian Newspeak, an inability to say what we mean, a condition of external dishonesty that inevitably leads to internal dishonesty. Orwell imagined the result of this to be something he called doublethink: people holding "simultaneously two opinions which cancelled out, knowing them to be contradictory and believing in both of them."

I find it difficult to imagine a better description of many of our TV talk show hosts—or much of our public discourse—today.

There are three main political positions we hear over and over in Pakistan, and all three are suffused with doublethink. There is the national security position: "America is our enemy; America should give us more aid." The privileged liberal position: "There should be equal rights for all; I should not have to share my riches with the poor." And the (remarkably similar) ambitious cleric position: "Religion makes us all equal; only I decide what religion says."

It is unsurprising that the privileged liberal position is the one most often associated with attempts to protect the rights of religious minorities in our country. It is also unsurprising that it has been largely unpersuasive.

The good news, from a religious minority standpoint, is that the other positions are equally incoherent. (The bad news is that they are much more willing to resort to violence in support of their arguments.)

What Pakistan's religious minorities need, therefore, is a new position, a position that champions equality while, and this is the tricky part, also championing equality. In other words, a position that dispenses with the illusion that equality can be enhanced in a society prostrate before either its rich or its clerics.

Such a position would also be to the benefit of the country's economic majority, its poor. For they, too, are looked down upon, discriminated against, physically threatened, and not infrequently killed. They, too, are second-class citizens. They, too, have been actively oppressed by our state.

At its heart, our country's toxic treatment of its religious minorities is intertwined with its toxic treatment of its impoverished majority. Both groups suffer from the denial of our common humanity. And that, paradoxically, offers great hope. For we can reject false dichotomies between our clerical and our liberal positions, between our minorities and our majority. We can begin the search for common ground that has eluded us as a nation thus far.

We might, for example, shift from disputes over blasphemy laws to actually delivering due process of law, from arguments over curbing radical madrassas to actually building a high-quality state education system, from alternately buying off and fighting tribal chieftains to actually empowering local tribespeople.

Our problems are not insurmountable. Pakistan is, simply put, a land that mistreats its minorities and its majority. It is ripe for a revolution, except that it already has many trappings of democracy: elected assemblies, free media, independent judges. A revolution in our thinking and behavior, brought about by sustained pressure from below, is what is really called for.

Let us be clear: the messy but effective compromises we require can only come about through the dramatically improved functioning of our democracy. But a better-functioning democracy is feared by many with vested interests who benefit from the impaired system we currently have. They must be convinced otherwise.

Above all, we must convince our powerful national security state. Rationally, it is clear that under our current policies, Pakistan is becoming ever less secure. The stability and growth that a well-functioning democracy could bring is our country's best chance of escaping from its "eagerly-dependent-on-enemy-America" strategic incoherence. Unless, that is, our national security doublethink really boils down to this: "I will protect you; you are the threat."

For the sake of our vulnerable, which is to say, in different ways, just about all of us, I hope this is not the case. Too much Pakistani blood has already been shed and too many Pakistanis have already gone to bed hungry.

(2011)

Osama bin Laden's Death

As NEWS OF terrorist leader Osama bin Laden's death reverberates in Pakistan, embassies here are shutting down, hotels are ramping up security, restaurants are reporting canceled reservations, and public gatherings like plays, concerts, and lectures are being postponed. The feeling in Lahore is familiar: it is like the dread that lingers over the city in the days after it has suffered a massive terrorist attack.

This time, though, the attack has not yet happened, and the dread spans the entire country. Pakistanis know they may pay a blood price for Bin Laden's killing. A purported mirror has been broken. Bad luck is to be expected.

Yet as I speak to friends and visit the market there is resignation as well. After a decade of slaughter, many here feel that terrorists are already striking Pakistan as hard as they can, and moreover that al-Qaeda is no longer as powerful as other militant groups. The most common sentiment I hear is that nothing much will change.

That depends, of course, on how the US responds. Barack Obama noted in his speech that "counterterrorism cooperation with Pakistan helped lead us to Bin Laden and the compound where he was hiding." But he also said that "a small team of Americans carried out the operation" itself. Between these two assertions is a gap open to a horde of questions.

For Bin Laden was not killed in the tribal areas near the Pakistan-Afghanistan border. He was killed in Abbottabad, a place I last visited a few years ago. In my childhood, Abbottabad was known as a pleasant hill station, a rest stop not far from Islamabad along the fabled Silk Road that winds its way to China through the mighty Karakoram and Himalaya mountains. Rampant population growth and climate change have seen its desirability as a tourist destination decline.

But while well-off Pakistani tourists no longer flock to Abbottabad as they once did, it remains famous in the country for its proximity to the Pakistan Military Academy, located just a few kilometers away. Hunting down a wanted terrorist in Abbottabad is, in American or British terms, like hunting him down near West Point or Sandhurst.

So a debate is raging in Pakistan over what really happened. Conspiracy theories abound. Some say that Pakistani intelligence agencies uncovered Bin Laden but wanted the US to take responsibility for his killing in order to blunt a possible backlash against Pakistan. Others argue that it is inconceivable that US helicopters could have penetrated so deeply into Pakistani airspace without being detected by the Pakistan army and air force (in the past, US helicopter incursions near the Afghanistan border have been turned back with warning shots), and therefore the operation must have been jointly authorized.

But there are other, truly frightening theories, such as that even in a town with as dense a military presence as Abbottabad, Bin Laden managed to elude Pakistani security forces, suggesting a remarkable degree of incompetence. More terrifying still would be if there were official complicity in harboring him, putting Pakistan on a collision course with the US. Pakistanis must hope that neither of these is true.

Because Pakistan is suffering badly. Crowds are justifiably celebrating Bin Laden's death in downtown Manhattan, where a decade ago al-Qaeda terrorists infamously massacred nearly three thousand people.

But since the subsequent US invasion of Afghanistan, terrorists have killed many times that number of people in Pakistan. Tens of thousands have died here in terror and counterterror violence, slain by bombs, bullets, cannons, and drones. America's 9/11 has given way to Pakistan's 24/7/365. The battlefield has been displaced. And in Pakistan it is much more bloody.

If Osama bin Laden's death means that the war in south and central Asia can now begin to end, that America can begin to withdraw its forces from the region, and that Pakistan and Afghanistan can somehow rediscover peace, then one day there may be celebrations here as well.

In the meantime American, Pakistani, Afghan, and terrorist commanders will go on conducting their operations, the slaughter will continue, and human beings—all equal, all equal—will keep dying, their deaths mostly invisible to the outside world but at a rate evoking a line of aircraft stretching off into the distance, bearing down upon tower after tower after tower. Bin Laden is dead. But many Pakistanis sense the impending arrival of yet another murderous plane, headed their way.

(2011)

11

Why They Get Pakistan Wrong

Why They Get Pakistan Wrong

NEARLY TEN YEARS after the terrorist attacks of September 11, 2001, and the commencement of the US-led war in Afghanistan, the alliance between the US and Pakistan is on shaky ground. The killing of Osama bin Laden by US special forces this May in Abbottabad, Pakistan, has incensed officials on both sides: on the American side because Bin Laden's hiding place appears to suggest Pakistani perfidy; and on the Pakistani side because the US raid humiliatingly violated Pakistan's sovereignty.

As Ted Poe, a Republican congressman on the House Committee on Foreign Affairs, puts it: "Unless the State Department can certify to Congress that Pakistan was not harboring America's number-one enemy, Pakistan should not receive one more cent of American funding." Dramatic words,*

---

*Indeed, perhaps more than just words: on July 9, 2011, the US announced it was holding back $800 million of military aid for Pakistan.

for Pakistan has been allocated quite a few cents of American funding. Yet this money has bought little love. According to the Pew Global Attitudes Project, only 12 percent of Pakistanis have a favorable opinion of the United States, and only 8 percent would like to see US troops "stay in Afghanistan until the situation has stabilized." Why might this be the case?

The past decade has been devastating for Pakistan. The country's annual death toll from terrorist attacks rose from 164 in 2003 to 3,318 in 2009, a level exceeding the number of Americans killed on September 11. Some 35,000 Pakistanis, including 3,500 members of security forces, have died in terror and counterterror violence. Millions more have been displaced by fighting. It is difficult to convey how profoundly the country has been wounded. In 1989, my Lahore American School classmates and I (including children from Pakistan, America, Canada, Sweden, Germany, and Korea) were able to go to the beautiful valley of Swat by bus for a weeklong field trip with no security arrangements whatsoever. In 2009, the battle to retake Swat from Taliban militants involved two full divisions of the Pakistani army and hundreds of casualties among Pakistani soldiers. (Similarly, until a few years ago, there had never been a suicide bombing in Lahore. Now one occurs every three or four months.) The Pakistani government puts direct and indirect economic losses from terrorism over the last ten years at $68 billion.

Of the $20.7 billion in US funding allocated to Pakistan from 2002 to 2010, $14.2 billion was for the Pakistani military. On paper, economic assistance came to $6.5 billion, less than a third of the total. In reality the civilian share was even smaller, probably less than a quarter, for the $6.5 billion figure reflects "commitments" (amounts budgeted by the US), not "disbursements" (amounts actually given to Pakistan). The United States Government Accountability Office reports that only 12 percent of the $1.5 billion in economic assistance to Pakistan authorized for 2010 was actually disbursed that year. Independent calculations by the Center for Global Development suggest that $2.2 billion of civilian aid budgeted for Pakistan is currently undisbursed, meaning that total economic assistance actually received from the US over the past nine years is in the vicinity of $4.3 billion, or $480 million per year. (By comparison, Pakistanis abroad remit $11 billion to their families in Pakistan annually, over twenty times the flow of US economic aid.)

Pakistan is a large country, with a population of 180 million and a GDP of $175 billion. Average annual US economic assistance comes to less than 0.3 percent of Pakistan's current GDP, or $2.67 per Pakistani citizen. Here in Lahore, that's the price of a six-inch personal-size pizza with no extra toppings from Pizza Hut.

The alliance between the US and Pakistan is thus predominantly between the US and the Pakistani military. To enter the US as a Pakistani civilian "ally" now (a Herculean task, given ever-tighter visa restrictions) is to be subjected to hours of inane secondary screening upon arrival. ("Have you ever had combat training, sir?") For a decade, meanwhile, successive civilian Pakistani finance ministers have gone to Washington reciting a mantra of "trade not aid." They have been rebuffed, despite a WikiLeaked 2010 cable from the US embassy in Islamabad strongly supporting a free trade agreement with Pakistan and citing research showing that such an arrangement would likely create 1.4 million new jobs in Pakistan, increase Pakistani GDP growth by 1.5 percent per year, double inflows of foreign direct investment to Pakistan, and (because Pakistani exports would come largely from textile industries that US-based manufacturers are already exiting) have "no discernible impact" on future US employment.

Perhaps the vast majority of Pakistanis with an unfavorable view of the United States simply believe their annual free pizza is not worth the price of a conflict that claims the lives of thousands of their fellow citizens each year.

PAKISTANI JOURNALIST Zahid Hussain, in *The Scorpion's Tail*, his examination of the rise of militants in Pakistan, makes clear that both sides of the alliance between the US and the Pakistani military share blame for the violence currently afflicting Pakistan. A long series of mutual policy missteps led to the present bloodshed.

As Hussain reminds us, the US and the Pakistani military together backed the Afghanistan guerrilla campaign against the Soviet invasion in the 1980s, thereby bequeathing to the world unprecedented international networks of well-trained jihadist militants. For the US, as in its previous alliance with the Pakistani military in the 1950s and 1960s, the primary objective was to counter the Soviets. For the Pakistani military, as ever, the primary objective of the alliance was to lessen India's superiority in conventional arms. The US gained a proxy fighting force in the form of the Afghan mujahideen (literally: "people who do jihad"). The Pakistani military gained access to advanced US-made weapons, the most important of which were forty F-16 fighter aircraft: too few, obviously, to resist any full-blown Soviet air assault, but enough to strengthen meaningfully the Pakistan air force against its Indian rival.

With the Soviet withdrawal, America turned abruptly away from the region and washed its hands of its militant co-creations; in the ensuing power vacuum Afghanistan descended into a bloody civil war among former mujahideen. The US also severed its alliance with the Pakistani military, cutting off supplies of spare parts for Pakistan's American weapons and withholding delivery of further F-16s that Pakistan had paid for but not yet received.

The outraged Pakistani military was seriously weakened as a conventional fighting force vis-à-vis India. But it now, as Hussain shows, had enormous experience of projecting power through jihadist militants and two opportunities to continue doing so. One was in the Indian-controlled part of Kashmir (the divided Muslim-majority territory at the center of the

Indian–Pakistani conflict, claimed in its entirety by both Hindu-majority India and Muslim-majority Pakistan), where an insurgency against Indian troops had broken out in 1989 following a disputed election.

The other was in Afghanistan, where the largely ethnic-Pashtun, Pakistan-backed Taliban were battling the largely non-Pashtun, India-backed Northern Alliance, consisting of Tajiks, Uzbeks, Hazaras, and others. During the 1990s, Hussain writes, "The jihadist movement in Pakistan was focused entirely on supporting the regional strategy of the Pakistani military establishment: to liberate Kashmir from India and install a Pashtun government in Afghanistan."

But following the terrorist attacks of September 11, linked to members of al-Qaeda living under Taliban protection in Afghanistan, the US returned to the region in force and demanded that Pakistan choose sides. President Pervez Musharraf's subsequent decision to align Pakistan with the US was perceived by many militants as a "betrayal." Still, Musharraf hoped the Pakistani military's conflict with its infuriated jihadist offspring could be circumscribed, that it might be possible "to drive a wedge between the Pakistani militants and the al-Qaeda foreigners."

This plan, besides denying the extent of the militant threat to Pakistan, was also undermined by US strategy, a strategy that suffered from the outset from what Hussain identifies as two "fundamental flaws." The first of these was a failure to understand that unless Pashtun grievances were addressed—

particularly their demand for a fair share of power—the war in Afghanistan would become "a Pashtun war, and that the Pashtuns in Pakistan would become . . . strongly allied with both al-Qaeda and the Taliban."

As the US campaign in Afghanistan began, Hussain writes, Musharraf "warned the United States not to allow the [Northern] Alliance forces to enter Kabul before a broad-based Afghan national government was put in place." But the US ignored this advice, and later, at the Bonn conference of December 2001, Hamid Karzai was installed as chairman (and subsequently president) as Pashtun "window dressing, while the Northern Alliance took over the most powerful sections of the government."

By backing the Northern Alliance against the Taliban and then failing to include a meaningful representation of Pashtuns in a power-sharing deal in Kabul, the US not only sided with India in the Indian–Pakistani proxy war in Afghanistan, it also elevated a coalition of Afghanistan's smaller ethnicities above its largest ethnic group, the Pashtuns. Conflict was inevitable, and since twice as many Pashtuns live in Pakistan as in Afghanistan, it was also inevitable that this conflict would spill over the border.

The results for Pakistan were catastrophic. Over the following decade, as Hussain describes in detail, the Pakistani military's attempts to separate "good" militants from "bad" foundered. Instead, strong networks developed between radical groups in Pakistan's Punjabi east and those in its Pashtun west. With each move of the Pakistani military against them, the frequency and lethality of counterattacks by terrorists inside Pakistan, on both military and civilian targets, intensified. Pakistani casualties soared.

THE ONLY WAY OUT of this trap, in which an unwinnable "Pashtun war" threatens to swamp an essential Pakistani program to neutralize militants, Hussain suggests, is to address the second "fundamental flaw" in US strategy: the "failure to appreciate that combating the militant threat required something far more than a military campaign," namely a "political settlement with the insurgents, requiring direct talks with the Taliban."

Equally vital, it must be added, is a push toward political settlement between India and Pakistan over Kashmir. This simmering conflict fuels the Indian–Pakistani proxy war between the Northern Alliance and the Taliban in Afghanistan, encourages the Pakistani military's embrace of militants, and helps subordinate Pakistani civilian governments to the Pakistani military (by allowing a near-perpetual state of security crisis to be maintained in Pakistan). The outlines of a deal on Kashmir were reportedly secretly agreed upon in 2007, but progress has been frozen since Musharraf's fall from power in 2008 and the terrorist attacks on Mumbai that same year.

As a presidential candidate, Barack Obama acknowledged Kashmir's central role. "The most important thing we're go ing to have to do with respect to Afghanistan is actually deal with Pakistan," he said in October 2008. "We should probably try to facilitate a better understanding between Pakistan and India, and try to resolve the Kashmir crisis so that they can stay focused not on India but on the situation with those militants."

Once he was elected, however, talk of Kashmir and peace between India and Pakistan receded from President Obama's official pronouncements, and he embarked upon an Afghanistan policy that might be described as "shoot first, talk later." US drone strikes in Pakistan's Pashtun belt intensified, with more—53—in 2009, Obama's first year in office, than during the entire Bush administration—42—followed by a further sharp increase in 2010, to 118. This unmanned assault was accompanied by a tripling of US military manpower in Afghanistan, which in turn resulted in a fourfold increase in the American fatality rate, with more deaths there of US soldiers in twenty-nine months under Obama (974) than in eighty-seven months under Bush (630).

Obama has now begun to reverse his Afghanistan escalation. His June 22, 2011, speech announced that 33,000 US forces (described as those of his "surge," but more accurately representing the second of his two roughly equal-sized surges) would begin withdrawing this summer and be gone by the end of the next. There will then, he said, be a "steady pace" of further reductions until by 2014 the change of mission "from combat to support . . . will be complete." He also stated that

"America will join initiatives that reconcile the Afghan people, including the Taliban."

The following day, in an interview with the Voice of America, Obama acknowledged a US "focus shifted to Pakistan" and declared:

> I think what's happened is that the [US–Pakistan] relationship has become more honest over time and that raises some differences that are real. And obviously the operation to take out Osama bin Laden created additional tensions, but I had always been very clear with Pakistan that if we ever found him and had a shot, that we would take it. We think that if Pakistan recognizes the threat to its sovereignty that comes out of the extremists in its midst, that there's no reason why we can't work cooperatively.

The tone of Obama's underlying message to Pakistan is certainly much improved from that of the US in September 2001, when Deputy Secretary of State Richard Armitage reportedly told Pakistan to cooperate with the imminent US campaign in Afghanistan or be prepared to be bombed "back to the stone age." But implicit in Obama's words, and explicit in his actions, is a continued willingness to escalate US armed intervention in Pakistan should Pakistani cooperation prove insufficient. The alliance between the US and the Pakistani military remains, therefore, a relationship between parties viewing one another through gunsights. Each side blames the other for putting its citizens in grave danger, and each is correct to do so.

A GUNSIGHT IS NOT, however, the primary lens through which King's College professor and former London *Times* journalist Anatol Lieven sees Pakistan. Quite the opposite: his *Pakistan: A Hard Country*, by far the most insightful survey of Pakistan I have read in recent years, reflects sensitivity and considerable, if clear-eyed, affection. Lieven has traveled extensively through Pakistan (dismayingly atypical for a contemporary foreign commentator), exploring all of its provinces and speaking with Pakistanis from a very broad range of backgrounds. He has also immersed himself in written sources, including pertinent anthropological research produced over a period of some two hundred years.

Pakistan's is a diverse society, so diverse, in fact, that observers who deal best in generalizations are bound to get the country horribly wrong. Lieven recognizes this diversity and makes it central to his analysis. For him, Pakistan is a place of competing and overlapping clans, sects, tribes, beliefs, and practices. Its society, in order to function, has evolved powerful mechanisms to deal with rivalries inside shared localities. As a result, Lieven argues, Pakistan is characterized by structures—military, bureaucratic, social, political, spiritual, judicial—that are profoundly "Janus-faced," in the manner of the two-faced Roman deity who gazes and speaks in opposite, contradictory directions. These structures, at once predatory and protective, operate to make the country both (frustratingly for reformers) very difficult to change and (bafflingly for forecasters of its demise) remarkably resilient.*

At the heart of Lieven's account of Pakistan is kinship, pervasive networks of clans and biradiris (groups of extended kin) that he identifies as "the most important force in society," usually far stronger than any competing religious, ethnic, or political cause. Several millennia of invasions, occupations, colonizations, and rule by self-interested states resulted in a "collective solidarity for interest and defense" based on kinship becoming paramount in the area that is Pakistan. It now, as Lieven points out, "is a cultural system so strong that it can persuade a father to kill a much-loved daughter, not even for having an affair or becoming pregnant, but for marrying outside her kinship group without permission." Moreover it is enduring, having survived, for example, "more than half a century of transplantation of Pakistani immigrants to the very

---

*Lieven is careful to point out that his analysis refers only to Pakistan as it has been configured for the past forty years, a territory with "more of a natural unity . . . [and] a degree of common history and ethnic intertwining stretching back long before British rule," and not to what he terms 1947–1971's "freak of history . . . [with] its two ethnically and culturally very different wings separated by 1,000 miles of hostile India," a situation from which Bangladesh should have been given a "civilized divorce" but which instead "ended in horrible bloodshed."

different climes of Britain." It has done much the same in the far less dislocating shift to Pakistan's cities, sustained, as in Britain, through constant replenishment by newly migrating kin from the countryside.

The effects of kinship on Pakistani politics are profound. Most of Pakistan's leading political parties are dynastic, including the Bhutto family's PPP (Pakistan Peoples Party) and the Sharif family's PML-N (Pakistan Muslim League–Nawaz); even individual members of parliament are often elected on the basis of clan alliances and support. Politics is therefore about patronage far more than ideology. Furthermore, the Pakistani state is relatively weak, collecting taxes that amount to less than 10 percent of GDP.

As a consequence, Lieven notes, Pakistani governments follow a predictable pattern. They are elected (usually as coalitions, Pakistan's many divisions making absolute majorities exceedingly rare) on general promises of higher living standards for the population and individual promises to particular politicians, families, and districts. The governments lack the resources to keep many of these promises (which are, in any case, often conflicting); their majorities ebb away; they lose power and await another turn.

Yet because of patronage, much of what politicians extract financially from official positions circulates among their kinship groups, which cut across class. Lieven believes this system, while hugely ineffective at driving real change, helps explain "Pakistan's remarkably low inequality rating according to the Gini Co-efficient, measuring the ratio of the income of the poorest group in society relative to the richest." By that measure in 2002 "the figure for Pakistan was 30.6, compared with 36.8 for India, 40.8 for the US, and 43.7 for Nigeria."

THE ROLE OF religion in Pakistan, a source of much hand-wringing in policy think tanks, is similarly complex. As Lieven points out, "the Islam of the Pakistani masses contains very different traditions." Moreover, unlike in Saudi Arabia or Iran, where an oil-bankrolled state has tried to impose one mono-lithic version of Islam, "the Pakistani state is too weak to achieve this even if it wanted to." Lieven describes the theo-logical divisions among Sunnis sustained by Pakistan's clan and kinship diversity. The Ahl-e-Hadith, heavily influenced by Wahabism, loathe saintly traditions. The Deobandis may praise saints but object to worshiping them. The Barelvis, Pakistan's most numerous (and "fissiparous") school, tend to embrace the intercession of saints with God. Veneration of saints is also central to Pakistan's Shias. Because saintliness can be inherited, the heads of Pakistan's powerful landown-ing "pir [saint] families remain of immense political impor-tance." They can actively create bridges among religious groups and they serve as major bosses in several mainstream political parties, especially the "secular" PPP.

Religiosity thus fuses with kinship networks and politics to reinforce Pakistan's existing elite. But it also helps marginalize Pakistan's Islamist parties, drawn primarily from the Ahl-e-Hadith and Deobandi schools, which struggle to capture more than a few percent of the country's vote. (Away from politics and "hardly noticed outside the country," Lieven believes Pakistan's religiosity also softens "the misery of Pakistan's poor" by contributing to an astounding level of charitable donation, which, "at almost 5 percent of GDP, is one of the highest rates in the world.")

Throughout his analysis, Lieven rejects the notion that Pakistan fits somehow in a category apart from the rest of the South Asian subcontinent, a sui generis nuclear-armed "failed state" on the verge of collapse. Rather, he writes, "Pakistan is in fact a great deal more like India—or India like Pakistan—than either country would wish to admit. If Pakistan were an Indian state, then in terms of development, order, and per capita income it would find itself somewhere in the middle, considerably below Karnataka but considerably above Bihar."

Indeed, even in the violent challenges confronting its state authority, Pakistan is like its subcontinental neighbors: "All of the states of this region have faced insurgencies over the past generation," Lieven notes, and by comparison to the Taliban conflict in Pakistan, Sri Lanka's Tamil rebellion "caused proportionally far more casualties" and India's Naxalite Maoist insurgency controls "a far greater proportion of India."

Lieven has evident sympathy for the Pakistani military (indeed there are points when, in referring to a uniformed ancestor who served during British rule in what is now Pakistan, one suspects Lieven may have his own feelings of kinship with the Pakistan army). But he is clear about the role the army has played in fomenting militancy, and about the deadly threat militants now pose to Pakistan, especially the potential for far worse bloodshed if the remaining militant groups that have not yet turned on the military and are therefore being kept "in existence 'on the shelf'"—including Pashtun militants focused on Afghanistan and Punjabi militants focused on India—were to do so.

Still, despite the ineffectiveness of much of the Pakistani state, he believes Pakistan's kinship groups and its stabilizing and antireformist social structures give the country a combination of diversity and toughness that makes successful revolution highly unlikely. He also writes that the Pakistani army, as it demonstrated in the "brutal but in the end brutally effective" operation to liberate Swat from militant control in 2009, is fully capable of routing guerrillas who seize territory when it sets its mind to doing so.

A key question, therefore, is whether the army itself could split. Lieven thinks not (and we must fervently hope that he is right). The army, he explains, is an all-volunteer institution with a strong shared ethos, nationalistic rather than pan-Islamic in outlook, and increasingly vigilant against Taliban sympathizers within—"after all, we are not suicidal idiots," an officer tells him. The real risk, which Lieven argues must be avoided at all costs, is of "open intervention of US ground forces" in Pakistan. For if ordered by their commanders not to resist, "parts of the Pakistani army would mutiny in order to fight the invaders," and in such an eventuality "Islamist up-heaval and the collapse of the state would indeed be all too likely."

In passages such as this, Lieven comes close to describing Pakistan as if through a gunsight; but the gunsight belongs to an American decision maker on the hunt, with Lieven playing the role of preservationist guide. The best Western strategy, he counsels, would "stem from a recognition that Pakistan's goals in Afghanistan are in part legitimate—even if the means with which they have been sought have not been"—and would "seek a peaceful solution to the Kashmir dispute, despite all the immense obstacles in both India and Pakistan." For in the end, "not even the greatest imaginable benefits of US–Indian friendship could compensate for the actual collapse of Paki-stan, with all the frightful dangers this would create not just for the West but for India too."

Lieven's is a vital book, with much wisdom in its advice for the West. But equally important, this detailed and nuanced survey offers Pakistanis a mirror in which to look hard at their country and themselves. Pakistan's resilience is bound up with its resistance to reform, yet reform will be essential for facing the great challenges ahead, including the potentially devastat-ing impacts of climate change on a dry and overpopulated land that is dependent on a single river and its tributaries. Pakistanis, and above all members of Pakistan's military, would do well finally to reject their country's disastrous embrace of militants. Pakistan must urgently mend its relationships in its own neighborhood and refocus on taking care of itself. Time is not on its side.

(2011)

12

Nationalism Should Retire
  at Sixty-Five

—

To Fight India, We Fought
  Ourselves

Nationalism Should Retire at Sixty-Five

M Y HOME COUNTRY, Pakistan, was born sixty-five years ago today. Next door, India reaches that milestone tomorrow. We're in crowded company, anniversary-wise: three-quarters of Asia's 4.2 billion people live in states that became independent or free of occupation around the same time, nations now in their sixties.

I would like to report that an aura of enlightened wisdom suffuses countries in their seventh decade. But, glancing around Asia, the years on either side of age sixty-five seem to bring instead an unfortunate obsession with national supremacy.

Pakistan, for example, is meddling in the affairs of neighbors, victimizing marginalized ethnic and religious groups, and building nuclear weapons while citizens go without electricity. India is doing the same. China is flexing its muscles along its frontiers, North and South Korea are growling at each other, and so are Iran and Saudi Arabia. Continent-wide, military spending is ratcheting upward.

Asian economies are approaching and surpassing in size those of Europe and North America. So it's worth asking whether Asian states also hope to approach and surpass in horror the nationalistic miscalculations of Europe and North America, mistakes that made much of the twentieth century a blood-drenched global battleground?

Many say that the twenty-first century will be the Asian century, that Asia will become central to the world economy and to global geopolitics. But for us Asians, the Asian century is also likely to bring a great dryness. Monsoon rains will become unpredictable and aquifers will drop, as is already happening in India and Pakistan. These changes could in turn unleash famines and provoke deadly conflicts over disputed rivers and watersheds, especially those of the Himalayas.

And the Asian century is likely to bring a great wetness. Sea levels will rise and low-lying land will be inundated, as is already happening in the Maldives. Billions of Asians live in coastal areas. The displacement of large numbers of them, on the strip between Chennai and Yangon, say, or between Singapore and Shanghai, could trigger movements of people so gargantuan as to be unprecedented in history.

The Asian century is also likely to bring a great aging, a great inequality, a great slum expansion. It is likely to bring challenges too big for any one of our countries, even the biggest, to tackle humanely alone.

It may, therefore, be time for us to recognize that aggressively thumping one's sexagenarian chest is a sign not of virility but of willful self-delusion. At sixty-five we would be better off thinking of retirement. Maybe not yet of our nations, for first we will have to develop a good alternative, but at least of our prickly nationalisms.

We need to begin to dismantle the chauvinisms we have built (partly as inoculations against the shame of our colonial experiences), and think about a morality that is bigger than Pakistan or India or even China—a morality that dares to be at least Asian in scale, and having achieved that, is ready to progress to something even larger, to the scale of humanity.

How might this be achieved? A change in rhetoric would be helpful. Instead of a relentless focus on the divided interests of our nations, the incessant drum beating of national propaganda, and the dice throwing of great games, we could begin to speak of an Asian interest, and a human interest, that is the opposite of zero sum.

We could commit to a blurring and reconceiving of national boundaries, to the immediate benefit of frontier-split communities, and to the growing benefit of everyone else. We might, as a start, embrace cross-border autonomous zones, visa-free travel, an Asian highway and railway network, and a reduction of legal differences between citizens and resident noncitizens.

And we could concern ourselves with a restoration of legitimacy at the global center, where the United Nations stands discredited. Instead of agitating for seats on the Security Council, we might push for its abolition, and for the creation in its place of a new, universal lower house with representation based on population.

The US and EU, despite the internal victories they have won for democracy and the rule of law, are stumbling on the world stage. Perhaps this is in part because their models are attempts at uber-nations, not at a post-national collective humanity. Such models are too small-minded for the challenges the globe faces, thrown off-balance by the conflicted ambition of mating individual equality with national superiority.

An advantage of wearing the hat of the largest continent is that, when imagining a system, you don't necessarily have to take as a starting point that preserving the advantage of the few against the many is in your own best interest. Asia is big enough to dream of a world where people are judged not by the color of their passport, but by the content of their character.

Our continent may still be a mess, but it is a mess with incredible potential. I say this from a room in a country that is messier than most, as my electricity supply cuts off every other hour, as my tap water remains unfit to drink, as foreign drones strike and local nuclear scientists toil, and as a group of boys who should be in school wander down my street, kicking what looks like a rusted can.

I hope for happier birthdays. For Pakistan, for Asia, for us all.

(2012)

To Fight India,
We Fought Ourselves

O N M O N D A Y , my mother's and sister's eye doctor was
assassinated. He was a Shia. He was shot six times while
driving to drop his son off at school. His son, age twelve, was
executed with a single shot to the head.

Tuesday, I attended a protest in front of the Governor's
House in Lahore demanding that more be done to protect
Pakistan's Shias from sectarian extremists. These extremists
are responsible for increasingly frequent attacks, including
bombings this year that killed more than two hundred people,
most of them Hazara Shia, in the city of Quetta.

As I stood in the anguished crowd in Lahore, similar protests were being held throughout Pakistan. Roads were shut.
Demonstrators blocked access to airports. My father was
trapped in one for the evening, yet he said most of his fellow
travelers bore the delay without anger. They sympathized with
the protesters' objectives.

Minority persecution is a common notion around the

world, bringing to mind the treatment of African Americans in the United States, for example, or Arab immigrants in Europe. In Pakistan, though, the situation is more unusual: those persecuted as minorities collectively constitute a vast majority.

A filmmaker I know who has relatives in the Ahmadi sect told me that her family's graves in Lahore had been defaced, because Ahmadis are regarded as apostates. A Baloch friend said it was difficult to take Punjabi visitors with him to Balochistan, because there is so much local anger there and violence toward the Baloch. An acquaintance of mine, a Pakistani Hindu, once got angry when I answered the question "how are things?" with the word "fine"—because things so obviously aren't. And Pakistani Christians have borne the brunt of arrests under the country's blasphemy law; a governor of my province was assassinated for trying to repeal it.

What then is the status of the country's majority? In Pakistan, there is no such thing. Punjab is the most populous province, but its roughly one hundred million people are divided by language, religious sect, outlook, and gender. Sunni Muslims represent Pakistan's most populous faith, but it's dangerous to be the wrong kind of Sunni. Sunnis are regularly killed for being open to the new ways of the West, or for adhering to the old traditions of the Indian subcontinent, for being liberal, for being mystical, for being in politics, the army or the police, or for simply being in the wrong place at the wrong time.

At the heart of Pakistan's troubles is the celebration of the militant. Whether fighting in Afghanistan, or Kashmir, or at home, this deadly figure has been elevated to heroic status: willing to make the ultimate sacrifice, able to win the ultimate victory, selfless, noble. Yet as tens of thousands of Pakistanis die at the hands of such heroes, as tens of millions of Pakistanis go about their lives in daily fear of them, a recalibration is being demanded. The need of the hour, of the year, of the generation, is peace.

Pakistan is in the grips of militancy because of its fraught relationship with India, with which it has fought three wars and innumerable skirmishes since the countries separated in 1947. Militants were cultivated as an equalizer, to make Pakistan safer against a much larger foe. But they have done the opposite, killing Pakistanis at home and increasing the likelihood of catastrophic conflicts abroad.

Normalizing relations with India could help starve Pakistani militancy of oxygen. So it is significant that the prospects for peace between the two nuclear-armed countries look better than they have in some time.

India and Pakistan share a lengthy land border, but they might as well be on separate continents, so limited is their trade with each other and the commingling of their people. Visas, traditionally hard to get, restricted to specific cities and burdened with onerous requirements to report to the local police, are becoming more flexible for business travelers and older citizens. Trade is also picking up. A pulp manufacturer in Pakistani Punjab, for example, told me he had identified a paper mill in Indian Punjab that could purchase his factory's entire output.

These openings could be the first cracks in a dam that holds back a flood of interaction. Whenever I go to New Delhi, many I meet are eager to visit Lahore. Home to roughly a combined 25 million people, the cities are not much more than half an hour apart by plane, and yet they are linked by only two flights a week.

Cultural connections are increasing, too. Indian films dominate at Pakistani cinemas, and Indian songs play at Pakistani weddings. Now Pakistanis are making inroads in the opposite direction. Pakistani actors have appeared as Bollywood leads and on Indian reality TV. Pakistani contemporary art is being snapped up by Indian buyers. And New Delhi is the publishing center for the current crop of Pakistani English-language fiction.

A major constraint the two countries have faced in normalizing relations has been the power of security hawks on both sides, and especially in Pakistan. But even in this domain we might be seeing an improvement. The new official doctrine of the Pakistani army for the first time identifies internal militants, rather than India, as the country's number-one threat. And Pakistan has just completed an unprecedented five years under a single elected government. This year, it will be holding elections in which the largest parties all agree that peace with India is essential.

Peace with India, or, rather, increasingly normal neighborly relations, offers the best chance for Pakistan to succeed in dismantling its cult of militancy. Pakistan's extremists, of course, understand this, and so we can expect to see, as we have in the past, attempts to scupper progress through cross-border violence. They will try to goad India into retaliating and thereby giving them what serves them best: a state of frozen, impermeable hostility.

They may well succeed. For there is a disturbing rise of hyperbolic nationalism among India's prickly emerging middle class, and the Indian media is quick to stoke the fires. The explosion of popular rage in India after a recent military exchange, in which soldiers on both sides of the border were killed, is an indicator of the danger.

So it is important now to prepare the public in both countries for an extremist outrage, which may well originate in Pakistan, and for the self-defeating calls for an extreme response, which are likely to be heard in India. Such confrontations have always derailed peace in the past. They must not be allowed to do so again. In the tricky months ahead, as India and Pakistan reconnect after decades of virtual embargo, those of us who believe in peace should regard extremist provocations not as barriers to our success but, perversely, as signs that we are succeeding.

(2013)

13

Why Drones Don't Help

Why Drones Don't Help

US DRONES OPERATED by the CIA first struck in Pakistan in July 2004. According to the London-based Bureau of Investigative Journalism (TBIJ), there have now been a total of 367 such strikes. These have reportedly killed between 2,541 and 3,586 people in Pakistan's Federally Administered Tribal Areas (FATA), the seven regions including North Waziristan and South Waziristan that border Afghanistan. The tribes on either side of the border were officially cut in two when the Durand Line between the countries was established in 1893, but in practice the border is porous. Of the 3.5 million people who live in FATA, most are Pashtuns, a group of tribes that claim common ancestry, divided into many subtribes and clans.

The frequency of US drone strikes in Pakistan has been strongly linked to US troop levels in Afghanistan. During the four and a half years that the drone campaign was conducted by President Bush, the American contingent in Afghanistan was typically 20,000 to 30,000 troops. Fifty-two drone strikes on Pakistan were conducted in this period. President Obama ordered a vastly intensified counterinsurgency operation that saw US troop levels in Afghanistan rise to 100,000. Under Obama's command, drone strikes on Pakistan likewise spiked to 315.

This link has been maintained since forces began withdrawing from Afghanistan in 2011. US drone strikes in Pakistan began diminishing that year as well: from a peak of 128 in 2010, they fell to 75 in 2011 and 48 in 2012. Nonetheless, the tempo of US drone strikes in Pakistan today remains considerably higher than it was under President Bush.

Living Under Drones, an excellent report by researchers at the Stanford and NYU law schools on the impact of US drone strikes in Pakistan, fails to give prominence to this declining number of drone attacks. (It was published last September, before full-year data for 2012 became available.) But it remains a vital and important document. The US government provides little public information on its drone campaign. The Pakistani government restricts journalist access to the tribal areas. Citizens of both countries should welcome the report's attempt to provide a rigorous accounting.

IF THERE IS any misconception that the drone strikes are primarily counterterrorist in nature, aimed at key leaders of international terror networks, this can be dispensed with. The report from Stanford and NYU highlights research separately conducted by Reuters and by the New America Foundation that comes to similar conclusions: the elimination of "high-value" targets—al-Qaeda or "militant" leaders—has been exceedingly rare, fewer than fifty people, or about 2 percent of all drone deaths. Rather, "low-level insurgents" have been the main targets of drones. The US drone campaign in Pakistan is thus largely a counterinsurgency operation, targeting men presumed to be intent on fighting US forces across the border in Afghanistan.

In the media, the term "militant" is often used in describing drone casualties. The report makes clear that this blurs together two legally very different groups of people. A "militant" who is a member of the Taliban, planning to attack US troops, is not the same as a "militant" who normally herds livestock, carries a rifle, and today is sitting with other members of his clan to discuss a threat to his isolated village from a neighboring clan.

Furthermore, according to the report, the "current administration's apparent definition" holds that any male of military age who is killed in an area where militants are thought to operate (and where, therefore, drones operate) will be counted as a militant if killed. This has allowed administration officials to make wildly unrealistic claims, disputed by even the most conservative analysts of drone casualties, that civilian deaths are "extremely rare" or have even been in "single digits" since President Obama took office.

If you disregard this novel definition and then try to ascertain what category of person was actually killed, you will arrive instead at an estimate that some 411 to 884 civilians have died in US drone strikes in Pakistan, including 168 to 197 children. These figures are from the Bureau of Investigative Journalism, which the authors of *Living Under Drones* determine to be by far the most reliable of the three main strike data aggregators (the others being the New America Foundation's Year of the Drone project and *The Long War Journal* of the Foundation for Defense of Democracies).

The report from the two law schools raises grave doubts about the legality of US drone strikes in Pakistan. In addition to questions around the program as a whole, specific practices are particularly troubling. These include targeting people who are not members of al-Qaeda or planning on fighting US forces in Afghanistan; so-called signature strikes, which involve attacking unknown people for gathering in groups or otherwise behaving like "militants," rather than attacking known individuals; and the use of drones against those who try to bring aid to injured victims of drone strikes.

The report also paints a harrowing picture of the experience of the ordinary people, among the most impoverished in Pakistan, who live in the region. Witnesses repeatedly speak of how the destruction of their house, the loss of a wage-earning relative with many dependents, or the need to borrow in order to pay for the treatment of injuries has left their families destitute after a drone strike. One of the interviewees, Ahmed Jan, who told the researchers that he used to work as a driver before he was injured in a strike, "woke up in a hospital in Peshawar . . . and learned he needed five to six lakhs (approximately US $5,300 to US $6,350) worth of surgery to implant a rod in his leg and stop the bleeding from his nose and face. Since then, he has lost most of his hearing and the use of one foot."

He can no longer work and relies on his sons to support his household. In his own words: "Before the drone attacks, it was as if everyone was young. After the drone attacks, it is as if everyone is ill. Every person is afraid of the drones."

Parents report taking their children out of school because of fears for their safety, and students speak of their diminished ability to concentrate. Social gatherings have been deeply affected, with many interviewees saying that "they were afraid even to congregate in groups or receive guests in their home." Accounts such as these, so rarely heard, serve as a reminder that the harm from the US drone campaign goes beyond the significant toll of civilian lives lost.

PAKISTANI VIEWS of the US have grown more negative in the years of President Obama's expanded drone campaign: 80 percent viewed America unfavorably in 2012, up from 63 percent in 2008, according to polls by the Pew Research

Center. US drone attacks have likely played no small part in this deterioration. Pew found that 97 percent of Pakistanis who were aware of the strikes were opposed to them.

Perhaps as a reaction, the Obama administration has recently tried to make drone attacks more discriminating. TBIJ calculates that the minimum civilian share of drone casualties has fallen from 14 percent in 2011 to 2.5 percent in 2012. But this is likely to be too little, too late. The US drone campaign continues to bedevil US–Pakistan relations, featuring prominently in the Pakistani media and in the statements of leading Pakistani politicians.

What we have witnessed is a perverse turn of events. The US began its military intervention in Afghanistan in 2001 ostensibly to reduce the risk of terrorist attacks on America. Today, al-Qaeda has largely moved on from Afghanistan, and US troops there are engaged primarily in counterinsurgency operations, not counterterrorism. Counterinsurgency is also the main objective of US drone attacks in Pakistan.

But these drone attacks may well be undermining counterterrorism efforts in Pakistan itself. And this matters greatly because extremists in Pakistan pose a threat to Pakistan, to its neighbors, and to other countries, including the US. The threat is especially pronounced for the people of Pakistan, where some forty thousand have already died in a dozen years of terrorist and counterterrorist violence.

Pakistan is far too big for outsiders to police. At 180 million, its population is almost three times that of the combined total of Afghanistan and Iraq, countries where recent foreign military interventions have proved less than successful. Also, Pakistan, notwithstanding its continuing corruption and manipulation of votes, has a democratically elected government, over one hundred nuclear weapons, and an army of six hundred thousand soldiers. The country must be responsible for dealing with its own extremist groups.

Fortunately, despite its frequent inclusion on lists of failing states, Pakistan is not a basket case. It has well-established political parties, noisy private media, and an independent-minded supreme court. It ranks among the largest global producers of cotton, milk, and wheat, and has over one hundred million users of mobile phones. Between 1952 and 2012, its annual GDP growth averaged 5 percent.

The main steps Pakistan needs to take in order to improve its situation seem clear: it should strive for a lasting peace with both India and Afghanistan; confront the extremist groups who kill foreigners abroad and Pakistanis at home, including Baloch, Ahmadi, Christian, Hindu, and Shia Pakistanis; and bring about a shift in spending from defense to investment in economically productive areas such as education and infrastructure (including water and electricity, which are both severely inadequate).

FREQUENTLY INVOKED as an explanation for the lack of progress in Pakistan is the intransigence of what is called a "deep state"—a secret, security-obsessed alliance between the Pakistani military, especially military intelligence, and militants such as the Taliban, along with extremist mullahs. Yet there are encouraging signs that the Pakistani armed forces may be changing. They recently adopted a new Army Doctrine that, for the first time, describes homegrown militancy, rather than India, as the "biggest threat" to national security. The document calls for a shift in training toward preparing for "sub-conventional" warfare against such groups instead of battling conventional armies.

Pakistani politicians, too, are showing increasing maturity. An elected government has unprecedentedly served out its five-year term, and new elections will be held in May. Despite a rocky economy and failures to improve security, parties from all the major factions have refused to back calls for a behind-the-scenes "soft coup" of the variety that has often derailed democracy in the past. Moreover, there has been improvement in relations with Afghanistan, where a groundbreaking deal for Pakistan to help train the Afghan army is being discussed, and with India, where the planned liberalization of trade and visa policies will hopefully still take place despite recent tensions between the militaries of the two countries in Kashmir.

Still, it is undeniable that Pakistan has not yet done enough to counter the extremist groups on its soil, whether the Taliban or others. To understand why, it is worth tuning in to the country's popular prime-time talk shows. There a reflexive blaming of, variously, the US, India, Israel, Afghanistan, Saudi Arabia, or Iran—anybody but Pakistan—for Pakistan's ills is, unfortunately, common. The result is a self-image of Pakistan as a pawn in someone else's game. To turn on one's TV in Pakistan is to find oneself entering a world permeated with conspiracy theories, an almost mythical space in which a refusal to accept that Pakistan can take the lead in solving its various crises seems not misguided but commonsensical.

The problem, for those who wish Pakistan to take more responsibility for itself, is that these conspiracy theories are not necessarily false. Indeed, many have elements of truth. India likely is striving to exacerbate the violent discontent in Balochistan, Pakistan's largest province, to the south of the tribal areas. (That discontent is rooted in the Pakistani state's long-term mistreatment of the province's local population.) Afghanistan has in fact refused to accept the territorial integrity of Pakistan. Saudi Arabia and Iran do back Sunni and Shia militant proxies in the country. The US has used a vaccination campaign as cover for an intelligence operation on Pakistani soil.

Conspiracy theorists have numerous examples they can cite in support of their positions. But perhaps none is as emotionally potent as the claim that flying robots from an alien power regularly strike down from the skies and kill Pakistani citizens. In the US, such a claim would be science fiction or paranoid survivor cultism of the furthest fringe-dwelling kind. In Pakistan, it is real. And constantly, wrenchingly, in the news.

Among the most pernicious aspects of the US drone campaign in Pakistan is therefore this: that it facilitates the refusal of the Pakistani state and Pakistani society to do more to confront the problem of extremists who threaten Pakistanis and non-Pakistanis alike. Pakistani politicians find it far easier to blame highly unpopular drone strikes for Pakistan's problems with extremism than to articulate concrete measures against specific extremist groups. President Asif Ali Zardari, whose government has endured heavy criticism for not preventing drone strikes from occurring, has said that "continuing drone attacks on our country, which result in loss of precious lives or property, are counterproductive and difficult to explain by a democratically elected government. It is creating a credibility gap."

Shahbaz Sharif, a powerful opposition politician, has driven his rhetorical dagger into this gap, claiming that Zardari's government, despite its denials, is actually helping US drone attacks. The popular cricketer-turned-politician Imran Khan, also lambasting the government for not stopping the drones, has taken an even stronger line. "These strikes have not reduced militancy," he has said, in views widely echoed by the Pakistani media; "in fact [they] have been a major stimulant to terrorism."

There was, of course, virulent extremism in Pakistan before US drone attacks began. There would be virulent extremism if US drone attacks ceased. But halting the attacks could quickly accomplish two things: end the obfuscating claim that drones are the cause of terrorism in the country, and make it less difficult for Pakistani politicians to advocate meaningful antiterrorism policies (rather than antidrone policies) without being branded lackeys of an America that regularly violates Pakistan's sovereignty.

WHEN FOREIGNERS intervene militarily in a region with disregard for sophisticated understandings of its internal dynamics, they tend, as recent history has shown, to fail horribly. The prevailing discourse in the West about Afghanistan and Pakistan is "simplistic, inaccurate, and alarmingly dehumanizing," to quote the editors, Shahzad Bashir and Robert D. Crews, in their introduction to the essay collection *Under the Drones*. The consequences, they find, have been tragic; and the chapters that follow make it difficult to disagree with them.

An essay by Amin Tarzi, director of Middle East Studies at Marine Corps University, reminds us of the many ways in which leaders in both Afghanistan and Pakistan have used the permeable and uncertain nature of the border between their countries to undermine the state on the other side. The Pakistani security establishment, he writes, has long considered that it is an advantage to have a weak, divided, and pliable Afghanistan. It has been tragically willing to back blood-soaked proxies, such as the Taliban, to that end. Less well known, perhaps, is that, since Pakistani independence, Afghan governments have refused to accept the location of the border. They have continued to maintain claims to Pakistan's territory west of the Indus—i.e., half of present-day Pakistan—and stoked Pashtun nationalism inside Pakistan by appearing to support the creation of "Pashtunistan," an independent homeland for Pashtuns.

By intervening militarily in Afghanistan, the US thrust itself into the middle of this border dispute without adequately recognizing it as such. As a result, two successive American presidents have repeatedly failed to get Afghanistan and Pakistan to take joint responsibility for security in the border areas. Tarzi is surely right when he asserts that "a rearrangement of Pakistan–Afghanistan bilateral relations, beginning with resolving the difficult question of the common boundary between the two countries, seems a necessary ingredient" for peace in the region.

One of several other remarkable essays is by James Caron, a lecturer on Islamicate South Asia at the School of Oriental and African Studies in London. He shows, through a historical examination of the expressive arts of the Pashto-speaking region, that the folk figure of the "talib"—or religious student, the singular of "Taliban"—is traditionally seen as romantic, antihierarchical, and opposed to the prevailing culture. There are obvious tensions between this folk figure and the present-day political-military group, but there are unexpected linkages as well. For instance, we read Caron's surprising description of the young Mullah Omar, now leader of the Taliban, singing classical songs called ghazals on the day he lost an eye during the campaign against the Soviets in the 1980s. One of the lyrics went: "My illness is untreatable, oh, my flower-like friend / My life is difficult without you, my flower-like friend." Caron suggests that such language allowed Taliban leaders to express their own "pious heroism" in terms familiar from courtly love poetry, and to construct a talib persona of "authoritative respectability" around their themes of "sincerity, earnestness, and morality."

Also arresting is a folk story, elaborated upon by Caron, of a young man named Talib Jan and Pashtana (literally: "female Pashtun"). In a recently printed version of this story, the two fall in love, but while the poor, low-born Talib Jan is away, Pashtana is persuaded by her unscrupulous family to marry her rich, high-born ("khan") cousin in London. Talib Jan dies of sorrow—pure, devoted to his love for Pashtana, and penniless—but after his death he comes to be venerated as a martyr. The story seems intended, Caron writes, "to convey . . . what is, for the author, the heartbreaking rejection of sincere talib morality by Karzai-era Afghan Pashtuns, and their 'marriage' to khan-ism through the intervention of foreign brothers."

The anti-imperialist and antihierarchical echoes of this tale are clear, and quite different from accounts of nihilistic militants belonging to a death cult at war with freedom—or, for that matter, of Pashtun supremacists bent on subjugating other ethnicities. Many of the Taliban have certainly proved themselves murderous, vicious, and Pashtuncentric. But their self-perceptions and the ways their motives are embedded in Pashtun culture do not necessarily correspond to popular caricatures in the West.

Most of the essays in this book—including noteworthy pieces by Sana Haroon, Shah Mahmoud Hanifi, and Faisal Devji—come across as challenges, intent on debunking popular myths. In his essay on the Red Mosque in Islamabad, which was raided by the Pakistani government in 2007, for example, Devji argues that it does not make sense to compare the aggressive activists of the Red Mosque with the Taliban and al-Qaeda. Many of the Red Mosque's practices that Devji cites are unknown among the Taliban, such as the involvement of women and their deployment as activists "shoulder to shoulder" with men. The experience of reading *Under the Drones* may, for many readers, be one of constantly losing their footing, as they realize that the assumptions on which their views are grounded have only tenuous basis in fact. It is a feeling that, over the past dozen years, US military planners in the region will have come to know well.

As DRONE WARS continue in Africa and Southwest Asia, we ought to remember that Western governments can be dangerously ignorant of these other regions. US policymakers are looking for a new approach to fighting terror after sustaining thousands of casualties in Iraq and Afghanistan. Drones do not expose their operators to the risk of physical harm and avoid the need for the large and costly deployments of troops with which the US public has grown weary.

So a widening and covert campaign heavily involving drone strikes might seem an attractive option. Already, the intensifying pace of strikes in Yemen (twenty-three in the second half of 2012) is on the verge of overtaking the reduced campaign in Pakistan (twenty-four in the same period). US drones have struck in Somalia, and there are plans to establish a base for US drones near Mali.

Yet to imagine that drone strikes are a panacea is to draw overly simplistic lessons from the wars of the past dozen years. Whatever the merits of toppling cruel and justifiably hated dictatorships in Iraq and Libya, these countries and their neighbors are today probably of more concern from the perspective of international terrorism than they were before.

Each country and region is different. But some states in Asia and Africa are trying to make transitions to democracy after years of despotic rule. During these transitions, they will often be weak. We ought, therefore, to reflect on the fact that strong states police themselves better than weak states. When states have elected governments, as is the case in Pakistan, and if the US drone strikes are unpopular, as they naturally are, the governments are likely to be made weaker, not stronger, by them. Few foreign military campaigns remain popular with locals for long.

Strengthening such countries will therefore depend on support for the complicated and unique internal political processes that can build in each a domestic consensus to combat extremists—who, after all, typically kill more locals than they do anyone else. International pressure and encouragement can help secure such a consensus. But it cannot be dispatched on the back of a Hellfire missile fired by a robot aircraft piloted by an operator sitting halfway around the world in Nevada.

(2013)

14

Islam Is Not a Monolith

Islam Is Not a Monolith

IN 2007, six years after the terrorist attacks of September 11, 2001, I was traveling through Europe and North America. I had just published a novel, *The Reluctant Fundamentalist*, and as I traveled I was struck by the large number of interviewers and of audience members at Q&A's who spoke of Islam as a monolithic thing, as if Islam referred to a self-contained and clearly defined world, a sort of Microsoft Windows, obviously different from, and considerably incompatible with, the Apple OS X–like operating system of "the West."

I recall one reading in Germany in particular. Again and again, people posed queries relating to how "we Europeans" see things, in contrast to how "you Muslims" do. Eventually I was so exasperated that I pulled my British passport out of my jacket and started waving it around my head. "While it's true the UK hasn't yet joined the eurozone," I said, "I hope we can all agree the country is in fact in Europe."

Six years on, a film inspired by the novel is in the process of appearing on screens around the world, and I am pleased to report that those sorts of questions are a little rarer now than they were in 2007. This represents progress. But it is modest progress, for the sense of Islam as a monolith lingers, in places both expected and unexpected.

Recently I was told by a well-traveled acquaintance in London that while Muslims can be aggressive, they are united by a sense of deep hospitality. I replied that I remembered being in Riyadh airport, standing in line, when a Saudi immigration officer threw the passport of a Pakistani laborer right into his face. If that was hospitality, I wasn't sure we had the same definition.

Islam is not a race, yet Islamophobia partakes of racist characteristics. Most Muslims do not "choose" Islam in the way that they choose to become doctors or lawyers, nor even in the way that they choose to become fans of Coldplay or Radiohead. Most Muslims, like people of any faith, are born into their religion. They then evolve their own relationship with it, their own individual view of life, their own micro-religion, so to speak.

There are more than a billion variations of lived belief among people who define themselves as Muslim—one for each human being, just as there are among those who describe themselves as Christian, or Buddhist, or Hindu. Islamophobia represents a refusal to acknowledge these variations, to acknowledge individual humanities, a desire to paint members of a perceived group with the same brush. In that sense, it is indeed like racism. It simultaneously credits Muslims with too much and too little agency: too much agency in choosing their religion, and too little in choosing what to make of it.

Islamophobia can be found proudly raising its head in militaristic American think tanks, in xenophobic European political parties, and even in atheistic discourse, where somehow "Islam" can be characterized as "more bad" than religion generally, in the way someone might say that a mugger is bad, but a black mugger is worse, because they think black people are more innately violent.

Islamophobia crops up repeatedly in public debate, such as over the proposed Islamic cultural center in downtown Manhattan (the so-called Ground Zero mosque) or the ban on minarets in Switzerland. And it crops up in private interactions as well.

In my early twenties, I remember being seated next to a pretty Frenchwoman at a friend's birthday dinner in Manila. Shortly after we were introduced, and seemingly unconnected with any pre-existing strand of conversation, she proclaimed to the table: "I'd never marry a Muslim man." "It's a little soon for us to be discussing marriage," I joked. But I was annoyed. (Perhaps even disappointed, it occurs to me now, since I still recall the incident almost two decades later.) In the cosmopolitan bit of pre-9/11 America where I then lived, local norms of politeness meant that I'd never before heard such a remark, however widely held the woman's sentiments might have been.

Islamophobia, in all its guises, seeks to minimize the importance of the individual and maximize the importance of the group. Yet our instinctive stance ought to be one of suspicion toward such endeavors. For individuals are undeniably real. Groups, on the other hand, are assertions of opinion.

We ought therefore to look more closely at the supposed monolith to which we apply the word "Islam." It is said that Muslims believe in female genital mutilation, the surgical removal of all or part of a girl's clitoris. Yet I have never, in my forty-one years, had a conversation with someone who described themselves as Muslim and believed this practice to be anything other than a despicably inhuman abomination. Until I first read about it in a newspaper, probably in my twenties, I would have thought it impossible that such a ritual could even exist.

Similarly, many millions of Muslims apparently believe that women should have no role in politics. But many millions more have had no qualms electing women prime ministers in Muslim-majority countries such as Pakistan and Bangladesh. Indeed, this month's Pakistani elections witnessed a record 448 women running for seats in the national and provincial assemblies.

Two of my great-grandparents sent all of their daughters to university. One of them, my grandmother, was the chairperson of the All Pakistan Women's Association and dedicated her life to the advancement of women's rights in the country. But among those descended from the same line are women who do not work and who refuse to meet men who are not their blood relatives. I have female relatives my age who cover their heads, others who wear miniskirts, some who are university professors or run businesses, others who choose rarely to leave their homes. I suspect if you were to ask them their religion, all would say "Islam." But if you were to use that term to define their politics, careers, or social values, you would struggle to come up with a coherent, unified view.

Lived religion is a very different thing from strict textual analysis. Very few people of any faith live their lives as literalist interpretations of scripture. Many people have little or no knowledge of scripture at all. Many others who have more knowledge choose to interpret what they know in ways that are convenient, or that fit their own moral sense of what is good. Still others view their religion as a kind of self-accepted ethnicity, but live lives utterly divorced from any sense of faith.

When the Pakistani Taliban were filmed flogging a young woman in Swat as punishment for her allegedly "amoral" behavior, there was such popular revulsion in Pakistan that the army launched a military campaign to retake the region. As my parents' driver told me, "They say they beat her because of Islam. This isn't Islam. Islam says to do good things. So how can this be Islam?" He offered no complex hermeneutics in support of his position. His Islamic moral compass was not textual; it was internal, his own notion of right and wrong.

I often hear it said, at readings or talks ranging from Lahore to Louisiana, that *The Reluctant Fundamentalist* is about a man who becomes an Islamic fundamentalist. I'm not sure what that term means, exactly, but I have a reasonable idea about the sentences and paragraphs that are actually present in the book. Changez, the main character, is a Pakistani student at Princeton. When he gets his dream job at a high-paying valuation firm in New York, he exclaims, "Thank you, God!"

That's it. Other than that exclamation (a common figure of speech), there's no real evidence that Changez is religious. He doesn't quote from scripture. He never asks himself about heaven or hell or the divine. He drinks. He has sex out of marriage. His beliefs could quite plausibly be those of a secular humanist. And yet he calls himself a Muslim, and is angry with US foreign policy, and grows a beard—and that seems to be enough. Changez may well be an agnostic, or even an atheist. Nonetheless he is somehow, and seemingly quite naturally, read by many people as a character who is an Islamic fundamentalist.

Why? The novel carefully separates the politics of self-identification from any underlying religious faith or spirituality. It sets out to show that the former can exist in the absence of the latter. Yet we tend to read the world otherwise, to imagine computer software–like religious operating systems where perhaps none exist.

And in so doing, it is we who create the monolith. If we look at religion as practiced in the world outside, we see multiplicity. It is from inside us that the urge to unify arises. A dozen years after 2001, we are perhaps getting better at resisting this impulse. But we still have a long, long way to go.

(2013)

ACKNOWLEDGMENTS

THE AUTHOR IS grateful to the nearly two dozen publications in which the pieces that constitute most of this book first appeared, in slightly different form.

"Once Upon a Life" and "Rereading" both appeared in *The Observer*. "Art and the Other Pakistans" appeared in *Hanging Fire: Contemporary Art from Pakistan*, edited by Salima Hashmi and published by the Asia Society in New York. "When Updike Saved Me from Morrison (and Myself)" appeared in *The Daily Princetonian*. "In Concert, No Touching" appeared in *Nerve*. "International Relations," "The Countdown," "Are We Too Concerned That Characters Be 'Likable'?," "Where Is the Great American Novel by a Woman?," "How Do E-Books Change the Reading Experience?," "Are the New 'Golden Age' TV Shows the New Novels?," "After Sixty Years, Will Pakistan Be Reborn?," and "To Fight India, We Fought Ourselves" all appeared in *The New York Times*. "A Home for Water Lilies" appeared under the title "I Love This Dirty Town" in *The New Statesman*. "Down the Tube" appeared in *The Independent*. "On Fatherhood" appeared in Pakistan's *Paper* magazine. "It Had to Be a Sign," "Enduring Love of the Second Person," "Osama bin Laden's Death," and "Islam Is Not a Monolith" all appeared in

The Guardian. "*Avatar* in Lahore" appeared in *TAR*. "Don't Angry Me" appeared on the website of *The New Yorker*. "Personal and Political Intertwined" appeared in *The Radio Times*. "Pereira Transforms" appeared as the introduction to the English translation of Antonio Tabucchi's *Pereira Maintains*, published by Canongate. "My Reluctant Fundamentalist" appeared in the "Original Essays" series on the website Powells.com. "Get Fit with Haruki Murakami" appeared in *The Atlantic*'s "By Heart" series. "The Usual Ally" and "Divided We Fall" appeared in the US and Asian editions of *Time*, respectively. "A Beginning" appeared in the *Frankfurter Allgemeine Zeitung*. "Fear and Silence" appeared in *Dawn*. "Feverish and Flooded, Pakistan Can Yet Thrive" appeared in *The Financial Times*. "Discontent and Its Civilizations" appeared in *The International Herald Tribune*. "Uniting Pakistan's Minority and Majority" appeared in *The Express Tribune*. "Why They Get Pakistan Wrong" and "Why Drones Don't Help" both appeared in *The New York Review of Books*. Finally, "Nationalism Should Retire at Sixty-Five" appeared in *The Times of India*.

Mohsin Hamid is one of the most inventive and empathetic narrators of our time

He writes with a finger on the world's rapid pulse and with keen feeling for its citizens. He portrays people deracinated by change, yet dreaming of their origins. He explores the clashes and commonalities of cultures and the individuals they contain; the pull of ambition and the sway of zealotry and corruption; the tug of migration and what it means to call a place home. A master stylist, he is a pioneer of form, with each new work creating a new way to tell the tale. He's tender and wry, sharply aware of shifting political currents, attuned to intimacies that link us all. He mirrors us back to ourselves, and enlists us— yearning, questing, and, in spite of everything, ardent for connection— in the story.

© Jillian Edelstein

MOTH SMOKE

A steamy love story, a noir thriller, a portrait of Pakistan in the throes of change

When Daru Shezad is fired from his banking job in Lahore, he begins a decline that plummets the length of this smart and darkly funny tale. Before long, Daru can't pay his bills, loses his toehold among Pakistan's elite, and, as if he wasn't in enough trouble, falls in love with the beautiful and restless wife of a childhood friend and rival. Desperate to reverse his fortunes, he embarks on a career in crime, only to find himself on trial for a murder he may not have committed—an uncertainty of fate that mirrors that of his country.

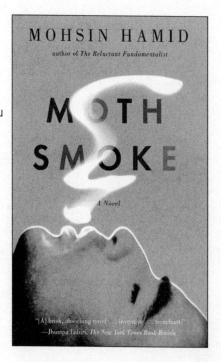

MOHSIN HAMID

author of *The Reluctant Fundamentalist*

MOTH SMOKE

A Novel

"[A] brisk, absorbing novel . . . inventive . . . trenchant."
—Jhumpa Lahiri, *The New York Times Book Review*

"A first novel of remarkable wit, poise, profundity, and strangeness . . . *Moth Smoke* is a treat."

—Esquire

"Stunning . . . a hip page-turner."

— Los Angeles Times

HOW TO GET FILTHY RICH IN RISING ASIA

The bestselling and unforgettable tale of a poor boy's quest for wealth and love

In a sprawling metropolis, a nameless hero begins to amass an empire built on that most fluid—and increasingly scarce—of goods: water. Yet our hero's heart is fixated on something else—the pretty girl whose star rises along with his, their paths crossing and recrossing over the years, a lifelong affair sparked and snuffed and sparked again by the forces that career their fates along. Stealing its shape from the self-help books devoured across the continent, *How to Get Filthy Rich in Rising Asia* creates two unforgettable characters who manage to find fleeting moments of intimacy in the midst of shattering change.

"Marvelous and moving."   —*Time*

"Extraordinarily clever . . . Hamid has taken the most American form of literature—the self-help book—and transformed it to tell . . . a surprisingly moving story."   —— **Ron Charles, *The Washington Post***